Quite possibly, no book in this decade has had as great an effect on American politics as **UP FROM LIBERALISM.**

Certainly none has caused ritualistic liberalism as much embarrassment. For in these pages what might be called the virus of contemporary liberalism was first isolated, stained and photographed.

Indeed, William F. Buckley, Jr., shows the affliction to be of epidemic proportions!

"THE SCOURGE OF AMERICAN LIBERALISM . . . RIDES AGAIN!"
—Arthur M. Schlesinger, Jr.
The New York Times

In a new preface—"That's the Way It Was, Baby" —Mr. Buckley reviews both the reaction to this book and the growing, grudging changes taking place in the liberal establishment today.

ABOUT THE AUTHOR

WILLIAM F. BUCKLEY, JR., editor of *National Review,* first provoked public attention with his best-selling book, *God and Man at Yale,* published in 1951. In it Mr. Buckley raised the urgent and searching question: What are today's students being taught? The book was probably the most widely reviewed of the year.

As editor of *National Review,* Mr. Buckley has led a team of the greatest conservative writers in America, including Whittaker Chambers, John Chamberlain, James Burnham, Willmoore Kendall, Max Eastman, Frank Meyer and Brent Bozell. The magazine has sought to revitalize the conservative faith, and has risen to the circulation level of its influential left-wing counterpart, *The New Republic.*

Mr. Buckley is a well-known and challenging speaker and debater who has lectured widely in the United States, and on television and radio programs.

Born in New York in 1925, Mr. Buckley spent years studying in England and France. He served in the Army during World War II, and entered Yale in 1946. He was chairman of the college paper and was graduated from Yale, with honors, in 1950.

UP FROM LIBERALISM

WILLIAM F. BUCKLEY JR.

Introduction by Barry Goldwater
Foreword by John Dos Passos

*This low-priced Bantam Book
has been completely reset in a type face
designed for easy reading, and was printed
from new plates. It contains the complete
text of the original hard-cover editioin.*
NOT ONE WORD HAS BEEN OMITTED

UP FROM LIBERALISM
*A Bantam Book / published by arrangement with
William Morris Agency*

Bantam edition published September 1968

Front-cover photograph courtesy of Editta Sherman

*Bantam Books are published by Bantam Books, Inc., a subsidiary
of Grosset & Dunlap, Inc. Its trade-mark, consisting of the words
"Bantam Books" and the portrayal of a bantam, is registered in the
United States Patent Office and in other countries. Marca Registrada.
Bantam Books, Inc., 271 Madison Avenue, New York, N.Y. 10016.*

PRINTED IN THE UNITED STATES OF AMERICA

To
Brent Bozell
James Burnham
John Chamberlain
Whittaker Chambers
Willmoore Kendall
Frank Meyer
—*mentors, colleagues, friends*

Contents

INTRODUCTION

by

Senator Barry Goldwater

THE RECENT RENEWAL OF interest in conservative principles was brought about, as far as I can see, not by the older members of the American community, but the younger. That is unusual; for the young are generally associated with the movements of the left, and it completely reverses the rule to see among the brightest young people in America, men and women who want to redirect the nation's destiny along conservative lines—individual freedom, local government, national sovereignty, and the religious view of life.

William Buckley has acted as a leader of this movement. He began, fresh out of Yale, challenging some of the basic assumptions of Liberalism in a celebrated book about the educational biases at his alma mater. He turned his attention to the problems of internal security in his second book, also a best-seller. Now, in this book, by far his best in my judgment, he delivers a stinging critique not only of the principles of Liberalism—or, perhaps, better, the "*no*-principles" of Liberalism—but of the behavior of some of Liberalism's principal architects. But however severe his indictment, which is deadly serious in intention, he does not forget to smile. And he doesn't lose his balance. There is in this book plenty of criticism of right-wing stodginess and shortsightedness, from which there is also much to learn.

This book of mind and heart, wit and eloquence, by the chief spokesman for the young conservative revival in this country, must be read and understood, to understand what is going on in America.

We have to thank Mr. Buckley above all for a readable and amusing and incisive account of the kind of people who are generally in positions of power today—in both politics and the academic world; and a penetrating view of the kind of world they seem to want.

The Liberals' world is not the kind of world I want to live in. If we are saved from it, among those we shall have to thank is the author of this book.

FOREWORD

by

John Dos Passos

THE FIRST DUTY OF a man trying to plot a course for clear thinking is to produce words that really apply to the situations he is trying to describe. I don't mean a fresh set of neologisms devised, like thieves' cant or doubletalk, to hold the uninitiated at arm's length. We have seen enough of that in the jargon of the academic sociologists which seems to have been invented to prove that nobody but a Ph.D. can understand human behavior. Plain English will do quite well enough, but the good old words have to be brought back to life by being used in their original sense for a change.

Only through a fresh approach, maybe through a variety of fresh approaches, can the terms through which we try to understand the events that govern our lives be reminted to the point of ringing true again. It is immensely heartening to those of us who would rather establish a true picture of the world we live in than one which is socially acceptable, to know that rash innovators are heartily at work. Thirty years ago the innovators called themselves radicals. Now mostly they call themselves conservatives.

The radicals of the period of the first of the century's great wars were trying to conserve something too. We were pretty concious of the fact that we were trying to conserve the independence of the average citizen which we felt the power of organized money was bent to destroy. This was the underlying theme of the Populist agitation, of the Progressive and Socialist and Farmer-Labor parties. Through the referendum and recall and primary elections and labor unions and cooperatives we thought that something like the old townmeeting type of self government could be revived. The aim of all the diverse radical movements of that politically fertile period was somehow to restore the dignity of the man who did the work. Staid Single-Taxers, direct action IWWs and bombthrowing anarchists had the same eventual goal. They believed that if every man could be assured of the full product of his labor, the Kingdom of Heaven would be installed on earth. Their quarrel was about ways and means.

The history of the twentieth century has been the history of a series of denials of these hopes. We can now see that the radical view was grossly oversimplified. It made no allowance, among other things, for the fact that man is an institution-building animal. In our enthusiasm for the "producer" we underestimated the importance of the planner and manager in industry. Marx had shrewdly pointed out the class solidarities which were so obvious in nineteenth century England, but he was too nearsighted to apply his theory of classes to human societies in general, instead of restricting it to the particular phase of the industrial revolution he had under his nose.

Though Marx's proletariat may be somewhat better fed than it was a century ago, its individual members have made little if any progress toward that personal liberty and independence on which the dignity of man is founded. Each new development of industrial society, whether under Communist dictatorship or under the mixed capitalist-socialist systems that have grown up in the western countries, has reduced the stature of the individual man. In the West he has been able to trade his liberties for some increase in material wellbeing. The American standard of living in particular has become the envy of the world; so much so that even in the Soviet Union the Communist masters have been forced grudgingly to try to match these capitalist allurements.

As the millennial dream of a perfect society recedes into a science fiction future, the slogans of its votaries become the liturgy of a new ruling class. Opinions of the sort that sent Eugene Debs to jail or ruined Thorstein Veblen's teaching career have become the accepted platitudes of the academic groves.

Forty years ago a young man in college spoke ill of businessmen at some hazard. Profits were a sacred word. Advocates of labor unions were jeeringly asked if they had ever met a payroll. The tenets of the free market economy were as much a divine institution as The Ten Commandments. With the devotion of young Mormons on their missionary year, college graduates took to the road to sell bonds.

How different is the climate in the schools today! An apologist of the profit system often finds it hard to hold his job.

When Business abdicated in 1929 it was not the working class who took over, it was the new bureaucracy. The radical theorists from the colleges crowded into Washington. They were in the driver's seat and they knew it. Whether their work was good or bad is beside the point. The functions they exercised established them as a managerial class. The First World War had enormously increased the power of the Federal government. Under Roosevelt the labor union bureaucracies took their place beside the bureaucracies of the great corporations as economically dominant forces. Then the Second World War left government towering over both. Class realignments went along with the increasingly hierarchical organization of society. When the old regime businessmen fell from their thrones, the leaders of a new class took their places.

The "liberal" mentality which Mr. Buckley puts over a barrel in this book is, I am beginning to suspect, the ideological camouflage of the will to power of this new ruling class. I can't find any other explanation of these fits of hysteria, these fixations which time will prove to have been irrational, some of which are so amusingly documented in this book. The Communists are excellent propagandists who have developed an uncanny skill in putting their words in other people's mouths, but they are not that good. Only some such phenomenon as the solidarity and esprit de corps of a class recently risen to power can account for the lynching spirit aroused against those who have sought to dislodge any fraternity member, whether bureaucrat or college professor, columnist or commentator, from an entrenched position of power. This disparity between the provocation and the reaction is, as the emotions of the moment cool, what stands out more and more as the characteristic trait of the "liberal." Here is perhaps a key to the subconscious springs of liberal behavior.

As the nineteenth century Englishman defended his home as his castle, the modern American bureaucrat will defend the security of his job to the death. For security he will give up fame and fortune. This is certainly true of federal office holders, but why should it apply to white collar workers so generally? Could it be that they too feel a solidarity with the ruling class as against the common run of anonymous citizens they seek to manipulate?

This is not Mr. Buckley's theory. It is mine. Maybe new developments will prove it to be worthless. In any case, the sort of high-spirited analysis offered in this book should prove useful to anyone who is working towards an independent appraisal of this midcentury phenomenon of "militant liberalism."

PREFACE

AMERICA, FASHIONABLE observers say, is a non-ideological nation; and it is understandable why this is a phenomenon from which one takes pleasure. No one is more tedious than the totally ideologized man, the man who forces every passing phenomenon into his ideological mold to end up, for example, concluding that every friend of Congressional investigating committees is an enemy of civil liberties, or that every enemy of Congressional investigating committees is a friend of civil liberties. American political conflicts are not generally fought on the battleground of ideas. The thoroughly non-Ideological Man is usually designated as steward of the American political community. This is partly a good thing, because everyone knows that ideological totalism can bring whole societies down, as it did Hitler's, and permanently terrorize others, as Communism has done. The danger comes when a distrust of doctrinaire social systems eases over into a dissolute disregard for principle. A disregard for enduring principle delivers a society, eviscerated, over to the ideologists.

America, most historians teach us, has sought to avoid the extremes, to be flexible without resembling Silly Putty; to be principled without being arch. I think our country is not clearly enough avoiding the former extreme. I think she is in danger of losing her identity—not on account of the orthodoxy that we are being told in some quarters threatens to suffocate us; but for failure to nourish any orthodoxy at all. I think the attenuation of the early principles of this country has made America vulnerable to the most opportunistic ideology of the day, the strange and complex ideology of modern liberalism.* I think, moreover, that disordered and confused though it concededly is these days, conservatism is the only apparent rallying point.

To put forward such a thesis is to take on many obligations. Very well. But bear in mind the logical maxim that one man's failure to prove a thesis does not render it invalid. I am by no means the ideal person to take on the job at hand, which is to discredit doctrinaire liberalism and plead the viability of enlightened conservatism. I have many disqualifications, among them that of having personally experienced the tenacious ill will of some of the men about whom I shall be writing; and I see some of them, day after day, berating people who stand for the things I love. I herewith hoist high a flag of truce, respectfully inviting their attention to what I have to say; but I will not feign surprise if the flag comes hurtling down, felled by a withering burst of fire from a hot-blooded evangelist in the liberal camp— who was brought up to assume that the differences between us, liberals and conservatives, are not negotiable. It is not as though the Communists had hoisted the flag: with the Communists, dialogue is altogether appropriate.

Who are the liberals? Numerically they are very few; for, as it is said, America is a non-ideological land. The average American is not "*a* liberal" nor is he "*a* conservative." He may have liberal leanings, or conservative leanings; but it is a mistake to think of him as a conscious agent, vocationally or avocationally, of any set of ideas. But liberals there are in the land, men and women who seek consciously and consistently to

---

* Throughout the original edition of this book, I capitalized the words "liberal" and "liberalism," by which I intended a pious gesture of historical deference to words that once meant something very different from what they have come to mean in contemporary American politics. But usage has now exhausted me, and I therefore yield them, lower case and all, to those who are in command of the meaning of the words.

advance a particular and identifiable view of man and society. They exercise great power (I cannot imagine a day's events free of their influence). I go so far as to say theirs is today the dominant voice in determining the destiny of this country.

Of these men and their ideas I propose to write. I mean to ask several questions about the liberal movement in this country, and to draw tentative conclusions from the answers that suggest themselves. I mean to ask first how the liberal thinks, how he argues, how he teaches, and then what are some of the root assumptions of his economic and political policies. I shall describe the behavior of prominent liberals in a concrete political situation a few years back. I shall describe the atmosphere is which liberalism thrives.

As to the conservative movement, our troubles are legion. Those who charge that there *is* no conservative position have an easy time of it rhetorically. There is no commonly-acknowledged conservative position today, and any claim to the contrary is easy to make sport of. Yet there is to be found in contemporary conservative literature both a total critique of liberalism, and compelling proposals for the reorientation of our thought. Conservatism must, however, be wiped clean of the parasitic cant that defaces it, and repels so many of those who approach it inquiringly. Up against the faith of a conservative, the great surrealistic ideologies reduce to dust. But first there must be a confrontation. The elaborate edifice of Marxism-Leninism crumbles before the poet's eye of Boris Pasternak; but the triumph of man over ideology remains confined to a poetic ballad, and there are those of us who are greedy to externalize the conditions of freedom and grace and faith that have sustained Pasternak in Hell. To do that we must bring down the thing called liberalism, which is powerful but decadent; and salvage a thing called conservatism, which is weak but viable.

Stamford, Connecticut, May, 1959

THAT'S THE WAY
IT WAS, BABY

Ten Years Later—A New Preface

To be exact, nine years later. When asked to write a preface to a new edition of *Up From Liberalism* I had a case of jitters at having to read back through asseverations almost ten years old. Needless to say there is a happy ending to that journey through fear, else obviously I wouldn't have brought the matter up. Very simply, it is this, that the case against the decadent liberalism observable ten years ago is much the same case one can make today, in the final period of the first term of President Lyndon Johnson. Indeed, some of the points stressed in this book which appeared at that time to some reviewers as at least a little bit over-tense, are points which are nowadays made by perfectly respectable liberals who, taking heed of history, find it opportune to stress that their relationship with liberalism has been rather contractual than conjugal, that they are not obliged to it in the sense that Mrs. Straus felt obliged to Mr. Straus, electing, in an act of gallantry which will live forever, to go down with him on the ghosted Titanic.

The purpose of *Up From Liberalism* was never adequately communicated by the title of the book, or at any rate such was the strenuous objection to the title voiced by Professor Gerhart Niemeyer, a conservative of deep perception and great historical convictions. His objection was that to designate a book as Up from whatever is to promise rather the vision of the new dispensation, than a description of the hell of the antecedent situation. Thus Booker T. Washington, whose *Up From Slavery* I unashamedly took off from, spent his time discussing the new life and opportunities of the emancipated Negro, rather than the horrors of his former state. I do not describe, at any length, the promised land of conservatism in this book. And even now, ten years after Professor Niemeyer's criticisms (which were echoed by a good many reviewers), I am, though always tempted to write a book about the good life, untempted to relate that good life to what automatically happens after one has excreted liberalism from the society's bloodstream.

My reluctance is to concede that the cogency of one's criticisms depends upon the subsequent cogency of one's affirmation (a logical and psychological non sequitur). To indict the law-breaker shouldn't require that the prosecutor define the good life. Beyond the disconnection between the one demonstration (that liberalism has failed) and the other (that "conservatism" is paradise), there is the additional point, that conservatives are obliged to deal in generalities, mostly of the non-gratifying kind, non-gratifying, that is, to schematic social thinkers (mostly liberal) who believe that one must in order to criticize a) be prepared to come out for b). What would *you* do about the poverty problem, Mr. Goldwater? What would *you* have done about Cuba, Mr. Burnham? What is *your* answer to the race problem, Mr. Buckley? One's answer to such questions, if one is a conservative, is either evasively aphoristic ("What role did you play during the Great War?" asked the boy of his aristocratic father in the legend of the twenties: "I tried to prevent the bloody thing"): or else it is melioristic, or even millenniarist. There is of course no "answer" to the "racial problem," and anything one would "do" sounds downright unconcerned, if not misanthropic: if not racist. ("I would do nothing," I said, when asked the question directly during the New York mayoralty campaign in 1965: "except promise justice.")

Mr. Russell Kirk wrote, several years before the first edition of this book appeared, a superb collection of essays called *A Program for Conservatives,* which continues in my judgment to be normative in the literature of imperative conservatism. But it is not a book the Platform Committee of the Republican Party is likely to consult when the time comes to describe its program in election year. And if it were, Mr. Kirk's book would probably not qualify as a true program for conservatives, the word "program" having been used by Mr. Kirk as a conscious act of disdain for the social engineers who tend to believe that our problems dissipate as they are reduced to politically actionable programs, the kind of thing one wins or loses elections by proposing.

More often than not, the conservative alternative to a liberal proposal remains its direct opposite. Let us go down to the sea again, to the lonely sea and the sky— does not require the naysayer to propose instead a visit to Howard Johnson's. A proposal that an end be put to the problem of Poverty by assigning the task of eliminating it, plus three billion dollars per year, to Mr. Sargent Shriver, does not require of the opposition a careful catalogue of better uses to which three billion dollars might be put. The "problem" of the conservative is less a philosophical problem, less—even—a practical problem, because the mere defeat of a particular liberal proposal can have a highly practical effect in forwarding a solution to the targeted problem by conservative means. The problem, actually, is ritualistic. It is a problem deeply involved in the ethics of modern political communication. It is said by some observers (e.g. Jack Jones in "The End of Thought"), that the Age of Euclid is behind us, that modern communication does not go forward by the old rules. Mr. Marshall McLuhan carried that observation further by his nowadays widely understood insight that the medium has become the message. Long before the insights of Mr. Jack Jones and Mr. Marshall McLuhan, the conservative knew that the demagogues had had their greatest victory by this means of impeaching their critics—on the grounds that they

had not "come up with anything better." Eric Voegelin*
pointed out that such arguments, brilliantly used by Pro-
tagoras, brought Socrates as close as he ever came to
doubting the possibilities of the dialogue in the absence
of certain rules. It remains to be said, now as ten years
ago, that the conservatives cannot compete program-
matically with the liberals, that to the extent that they
do (Repeal rent controls! Abolish the minimum wage
law!) they are forced into apologetic corners; that therefore the conservatives must dwell mostly on the failures
of the millenniarists, and take their satisfactions from the
essentially un-exhilarating experience of I-told-you-so's.
Which is another way of saying: Don't do it again.

There is, if one really wants to look for it, a metaphysics of conservative opposition. The liberals who gad
about claiming to find no philosophical depth in the
conservative position, are best neutralized by quoting a
few sentences from Professor Michael Oakeshott of the
London School of Economics who, by a masterstroke
of irony, occupies there the seat left vacant on the death
of Harold Laski. Mr. Oakeshott observes (in *Rational-
ism and Politics,* 1962), having first warned that ration-
alism is "making politics as the crow flies," that "To
some people 'government' appears as a vast reservoir
of power which inspires them to dream of what uses
might be made of it. They have favorite projects, of
various dimensions, which they sincerely believe are for
the benefit of mankind, and to capture this source of
power, if necessary to increase it, and to use it for imposing their favorite projects upon their fellows, is what
they understand as the adventure of governing men.
They are, thus, disposed to recognize government as an
instrument of passion: the art of politics is to inflame
and direct desire."

"Now"—Oakeshott explains—"the disposition to be
conservative in respect of politics reflects a quite different view of the activity of governing. The man of this

---

* *Freedom and Serfdom, An Anthology of Western Thought,* edited
by Albert Humold (D. Reidel, Dordrecht, Holland, 1961).

disposition understands it to be the business of a government not to inflame passion and give it new objects to feed upon; but to inject into the activities of already too passionate men an ingredient of moderation; to restrain, to deflate, to pacify and to reconcile; not to stoke the fires of desire, but to damp them down. And all this, not because passion is vice and moderation virtue, but because moderation is indispensable if passionate men are to escape being locked in an encounter of mutual frustration.

"Where activity is bent upon enterprise"—Oakeshott brings his analysis to a sublime analytical climax—"the indispensable counterpart is another order of activity, bent upon restraint, which is unavoidably corrupted (indeed, altogether abrogated) [Mr. Oakeshott's sudden departure here from the rhythm of his analysis suggests that he had to pause to reckon with the Supreme Court of the United States] when the power assigned to it is used for advancing favorite projects. An umpire who at the same time is one of the players is no umpire; rules about which we are not disposed to be conservative are not rules but incitements to disorder; the conjunction of dreaming and ruling generates tyranny."

2.

Other criticisms of *Up From Liberalism* are interesting. Several reviewers echoed the point of Mr. Arthur Schlesinger who, in the New York *Times,* first quoted from the definition of the liberal used in this book as someone who believes "that the human being is perfectible, and social progress predictable," that "social and individual differences, if they are not rational, are objectionable, and should be scientifically eliminated"— "I don't want to spoil Mr. Buckley's fun," said Mr. Schlesinger who deserves few things more, "but I myself don't happen to believe any of these things."

Mr. Schlesinger's dissociation from the credenda of liberalism is more heartening than convincing. A hundred years ago John Stuart Mill defended among other things the universal franchise on the assumption that the world about him had attained, in the generality, to that state of reason which justified the conviction that the majority would use the franchise for the commonweal: that—it was an inevitable deduction from his reasoning—things would therefore inevitably improve. Mr. Harry Jaffa (see his brilliant essay, "On the Nature of Civil and Religious Liberty," in *The Conservative Papers*, 1964) observes that Mill simply had no notion of what was in store for humankind, that the advent of Hitler and Stalin shattered the rationalist optimism which, although its extremist formulation is now disdained by such as Mr. Schlesinger, nevertheless continues to animate contemporary liberalism, with its faith in the universal franchise (Mr. Schlesinger does not raise his voice against the travesties in Black Africa), permissive egalitarianism (pity the poor of Watts, who *had* to riot), and the old epistemological relativism (Mr. Schlesinger is ever the champion of Oliver Wendell Holmes and John Dewey).

If, along with Mr. Schlesinger, liberalism is reshaping itself, and there are indeed signs that it is, and they are more abundant now than at the time this book was first published, then the entire world stands to benefit, and it would be pettifogging to remind those who carefully draw up their skirts from contact with the old positions and their old apostles, that they all grew up together in intimate communion. In another ten years, who knows, Mr. Schlesinger may make considerable progress, taking the lead from Mr. Patrick Moynihan and Mr. Richard Goodwin, both of them ardent and self-proclaimed liberals of the schools of F.D.R., and J.F.K., who now speak about the rational limits of politics, about the hubris of centralized power, about the failures of canonical liberalism to help the race question or do much about poverty.*

---

* See e.g. Moynihan, *Beyond the Melting Pot*, 1963; *The Moynihan Report*, 1965; "'The Moynihan Report' and Its Critics," *Commentary*, February 1967; and Richard Goodwin, "The Shape of American Politics," *Commentary*, June 1967.

Mr. Schlesinger, reviewing this book in 1960, saw signs that I was mellowing. I acknowledge his compliment by observing that if I continue to mellow much further, Mr. Schlesinger may find himself a conservative, battling, as Senator Bobby now does, for private enterprise to solve the housing shortage; or, as the Postmaster General, Mr. Larry O'Brien, is now doing, a mere five years after his patron John F. Kennedy teased Barry Goldwater for proposing the repatriation of the TVA to private enterprise, advocating that the administration of the Post Office be given over to free enterprise.

3.

A number of reviewers criticized this book when it first appeared for unconvincing faults. The book gives evidence against the behavior, persistently uncriticized, of such as the late Mrs. Roosevelt and Elmer Davis, Archibald MacLeish and Joseph L. Rauh Jr., Richard Rovere and Arthur Schlesinger. Reviewers suddenly found themselves without the appetite to defend those who, in their workaday rhetoric, they had always embraced as their very own. Most of them took the easiest way out—the way of Simon Peter: they simply dissociated themselves from such spokesmen for liberalism as I photographed in this book in embarrassing postures. Indeed I was treated by some reviewers as a voyeur, for having read the altogether public pronouncements of some of these ladies and gentlemen (an interesting question: do good manners require us not to look when a ritualistic liberal is speaking?). Mr. William V. Shannon of the New York *Post* said that I had picked on "straw men," which is not what Mrs. Roosevelt, Archibald MacLeish et al. thought of themselves as being. Mr. John Cogley, then of *Commonweal,* now with Dr. Robert Hutchins (itself an argument against Couéism), was (characteristically) the most courageous of the lot. He admitted that ". . . the weaknesses that Mr. Buckley finds in liberalism are genuine flaws, and I think he has proved that conclusively . . . there are sections in

[this] book which every man who calls himself a liberal should take seriously"—but then picked himself up from abjection by the tu quoqueism that conservatives are Just As Bad, rejecting, without exactly explaining why, the point I make (p. 8) that one judges a movement not merely by the deeds of its qualified spokesmen, but also by their acceptance as spokesmen by the larger community of the faithful.

It was Mr. Murray Kempton who made the criticism most shrewdly. He was not satisfied to make the point that I poke at straw men (he is too rigorous a sport to refuse to acknowledge that the most bumptious liberal polemicists are here repulsed); nor even to make the point other liberal reviewers made tauntingly, the same point Mr. Russell Kirk made most invitingly in his review of my subsequent book *Rumbles Left and Right,* that I should take on not the contemporary lilliputians, but their seminal antecedents: John Dewey and O. W. Holmes, J. S. Mill and Charles Darwin, Auguste Comte and Rousseau—hell, John Wycliffe and William of Occam while I am at it—but (Mirror, mirror on the wall/ Kempton's the shrewdest of them all) the tantalizing point that in this book I did not even bother to fire the Big Berthas available to a conservative polemicist. He adroitly suggested that this indicates either my ignorance of the weapons at my disposal, or my isolation from my own main army, namely the great historical and religious traditions nowadays thought to be quite adequately represented in the works of "Freud, Marx, Henry Ford, the Reverend Daniel Poling, and Edward L. Bernays." "[Buckley] is not a man widely credited with sportsmanship," he began characteristically, "yet which of his enemies could claim a single act so gallant as this immense forfeiture?" Well, this isn't a book about the lives of Aristotle and Augustine, Thomas Aquinas and Locke, Edmund Burke and/or Adam Smith. It is a book about our time, and about some of the political and philosophical presumptions of people who live together uneasily because they are animated by different presumptions, political and philosophical. I most heartily acknowledge the limitations of this book so judged, and I especially acknowledge what Mr. Kempton described as "the transient character of this book" on the tenth anniversary of its publication. I do truly hope, and I do truly expect, that in another ten years, events will have moved so as to confirm that we have come up from liberalism, and that only historical voyeurs will want to study the reasons why, as given, some of them, in this little volume.

A specific matter. I have gone over the original edition sentence by sentence. I have corrected the anachronisms, changed the tenses where appropriate, once or twice entered substantial clarifications. I have caught (to my horror) dreadful typographical, syntactical, and errors of other sorts (e.g. sentences entirely missing, or garbled) which were apparently the result of a reckless haste in publishing the original edition.

I was tempted to excise whole passages that related to Mr. Dwight Eisenhower, but did not do so because although Mr. Eisenhower is nowhere a fighting word these days, he was one during the late fifties, and it is appropriate that a book written in 1959 should reflect the fact that he was. In 1959 there was a most general dissatisfaction among conservative observers at the General's record as President. A dissatisfaction one does not, for reasons humanitarian and not in the least analytical, really take any pleasure in pressing at this moment. The same is so of Mr. Harry Truman: there are those who thought him a most unsatisfactory President; those who, if the straps of the polygraph machine were even now applied, would betray their continuing conviction that they were right the first time; who nevertheless would go out of their way *not* to make the point. But I have left unaltered, notwithstanding my knowledge that they will jar the modern sensibilities, the accents of total exasperation with which we viewed the doings and nondoings of Mr. Eisenhower during the fifties, during Suez and Budapest, during the Spirits of Geneva and Camp David. Mr. Eisenhower is nowadays viewed, by those who take refuge from the hecticities of the New Frontier and the Great Society, as the Raggedy Ann of yesteryear, the warm puppy of the cuddly past when the White House was occupied by competent bridge-playing businessmen, rather than ideological scriveners staying up late writing new laws for us to obey.

I wish, for the sake of plausibility, that I had recast the sections on Mr. Eisenhower, inasmuch as I know that I will lose, rather than he, by invoking the impatient tones of yesterday. But—that is how it was. That is how we thought and spoke about D.D.E. That is how we thought and spoke about Mrs. Eleanor Roosevelt. The offense at this point is not, in my judgment, that that was how we viewed them. The offense is purely a matter of taste, that—the matter presumably falling within our technical competence to prevent—we permit today the full ventilation of aggravated responses which were utterly spontaneous when they were uttered, but seem today to be unnecessarily overwrought. All I can say is that I thought about it: and decided for reasons which are obvious (and need not therefore be elaborated) and which are not obvious (and perhaps shouldn't be made so), to re-issue *Up From Liberalism,* rather than to re-write it with reference to the current state of political sensibilities.

Stamford, Connecticut, January 15, 1968

Up from Liberalism

I
THE FAILURE OF CONTEMPORARY AMERICAN LIBERALISM

"CONSTRUCTIVE CRITICISM. The demand for *constructive* rather than *destructive criticism* (usually with an exaggerated emphasis on the first syllable of each adjective) has become one of the cant phrases of the day. It is true that under the guise of criticism mockery and hatred often vent their spite, and what professes to be a fair and even helpful analysis of a situation or policy is sometimes a malignant attack. But the proper answer to that is to expose the malignance and so point out that it is not criticism at all. Most whining for *con*structive rather than *de*structive criticism is a demand for unqualified praise, an insistence that no opinion is to be expressed or course proposed other than the one supported by the speaker. It is a dreary phrase, avoided by all fairminded men."

From: *A Dictionary of Contemporary American Usage* by BERGEN EVANS and CORNELIA EVANS (Random House, 1957)

THE LIBERAL—In Controversy

THE MANIA

THIS BOOK IS ABOUT the folklore of American liberalism. I am very much surprised that so little of an orderly kind has been written about the American liberal. A good library will direct you to a vast literature on the history of liberalism, and every year or so a new book is published which presents itself as a hot-off-the-press examination of contemporary liberalism. But one who reads the literature, and then turns to look at the land he lives in, will have a difficult time reconciling the lofty presumptions of unleavened liberalism with the behavior and attitudes of liberalism's most conspicuous exponents.

There are always such discrepancies, let us hasten to grant—the bigoted churchman, the protectionist free enterpriser, the provincial internationalist, the licentious moralist—all of them well-known anomalies, widely commented upon in our literature. Yet for reasons that are persisting but hard to pin down, there is no sociological study of American liberalism. Is this because no *Middletown* could be written about the world of the Americans for Democratic Action? Or is it that the topic —the behavior and thought pattern of the opinion-makers of the most powerful country on earth—does not merit such treatment? Why should it be easier to understand the mind of Nikita Khrushchev than that of Chester Bowles?

A reviewer of my most recent book charged that it is

clear from my use of the word "liberal" that I could only have in mind the clientele of the *Nation* Magazine. I am encouraged that that reviewer, writing in a prominent liberal daily, tacitly conceded that the *Nation*-reader has recognizable spots, a concession that is very late in coming. I detect a little discomfort, here and there, when the word "liberal" is bandied about. Many people are not satisfied to be unique merely in the eyes of God, and spend considerable time in flight from any orthodoxy. Some make a profession of it, and end up, as for instance the critic Dwight Macdonald has, with an intellectual and political career that might have been painted by Jackson Pollock. But even discounting that grouping, an increasing number of persons are visibly discomfited by the appellation "liberal," and it can only be because there is in fact perceptible, even though the proper prisms for viewing it have not been ground, a liberal virus—and a corresponding liberal syndrome; things, surely, that should be written about.

The liberals I shall refer to in this book are men and women who are clearly associated with the liberal movement in America, however often they seem to be deviating to right or left from the mainstream. Because liberalism has no definitive manifesto, one cannot say, prepared to back up the statement with unimpeachable authority, that such-and-such a man or measure is "liberal." But one can say that Mrs. Roosevelt was a liberal, and do so confident that no one will contradict him. And say the same of Arthur Schlesinger Jr. and Joseph L. Rauh and James Wechsler and Richard Rovere and Alan Barth and Agnes Meyer and Edward R. Murrow and Chester Bowles, Hubert Humphrey, Averell Harriman, Adlai Stevenson, Paul Hoffman. The *New Republic* is liberal, so is the *Washington Post,* the *St. Louis Post-Dispatch,* the *Minneapolis Tribune;* much of the *New York Times, all* of the *New York Post,* save that oasis in which it publishes my dispatches. These men and women and institutions share premises and attitudes, show common reactions, enthusiasms and aversions, and

6

display an empirical solidarity in thought and action, on the strength of which society has come to know them as "liberals." They are men and women who tend to believe that the human being is perfectible and social progress predictable, and that the instrument for effecting the two is reason; that truths are transitory and empirically determined; that equality is desirable and attainable through the action of state power; that social and individual differences, if they are not rational, are objectionable, and should be scientifically eliminated; that all peoples and societies should strive to organize themselves upon a rationalist and scientific paradigm.

One asks: are there characteristic idiosyncrasies of the liberal mind at work? I think there are. Here we must draw an important distinction. Some minds are not trained to think logically under any circumstances. Miss Dorothy Sayers was much concerned about this as a characteristic failing of our generation which has nothing to do with ideological affiliation.* I shall not, here, be contending what Miss Sayers, whose dismay is shared by many observers of American education, contends, namely that the faculty for logical thought is a skill of which the entire contemporary generation has been bereft; I note, but do not press the point.

I shall be assuming that in most respects the liberal ideologists are, like Don Quixote, wholly normal, with fully developed powers of thought, that they see things as they are, and live their lives according to the Word; but that, like Don Quixote, whenever anything touches upon their mania, they become irresponsible. Don Quixote's mania was knight-errantry. The liberals' mania is their ideology.** Deal lightly with any precept of knight-errantry, and you might find, as so many inno-

---

* See "The Lost Tools of Learning," E. T. Heron & Co., Ltd., London, 1948.
** Mania (Webster): ". . . characterized by disorderly speech and thinking, by impulsive movements, and by excessive emotion." I shall be most grateful to any reviewer who resists the temptation to write: "The thesis of Mr. Buckley's book is that all liberals are maniacs."

cent Spaniards did, the Terror of La Mancha hurtling toward you. Cross a liberal on duty, and he becomes a man of hurtling irrationality.

The problems of demonstration are considerable, since I level my charge not merely at specific individuals, but at the disciples, en bloc, of a politico-philosophical movement. One can say, "Disciples of Communism, en bloc, follow the Moscow line." That is a responsible generalization, unaffected by the fact of schismatic flare-ups or deviationist sallies. Such a statement is not supported by counting the noses of all the Communists who have switched their positions to harmonize with a change in the Moscow line. This type of census is impractical. Rather, one observes the shifting pronouncements of Communist spokesmen and their house organs, and waits to see if substantial opposition develops from the rank and file. If it does not, the rank and file can be assumed to have complied—whether by internal assent or as a matter of discipline is irrelevant.

If one sets out to show that a religious sect is corrupt, it does not suffice to point to a member of that sect who has been caught channeling money from the collection plate to his mistress. *He* is proved corrupt, but not, yet, the movement. Suppose, then, one approaches the delinquent's co-religionists and asks them for an expression of opinion on the behavior of their brother. If they show a marked indifference to it, if they actively defend him, if they continue to countenance or even move him up the ladder of their hierarchy, more and more one is entitled to generalize—as in passing judgment on the union of Mr. James Hoffa—that the organization is corrupt.

How does one, then, go about demonstrating that the mania I speak of afflicts the spokesmen of a contemporary political movement? By these means, I suggest: by citing instances of intellectual or moral irresponsibility which, taken by themselves, would serve merely to demonstrate the limitations of the person under consideration; but which take on a much broader meaning if— and here is the critical distinction I make here and in other chapters in this book—the subject's publicly observed irresponsibilities *do not have the effect* of blemishing his public reputation among his factional associates.

I offer below a small cluster of illustrations, all but one in some way turning on the controversy surrounding Senator McCarthy. I go back several years for good reason. Whatever else Senator McCarthy did, he brought liberalism to a boil. Everything he did that was good, everything that he did that was bad, added together, do not have the residual sociological significance for our time of what his enemies were revealed as seeing fit to do in opposing him. Let us concede that if ever a man in America crossed the liberal ideology, or at least gave the impression of doing so, McCarthy did, which is why the McCarthy years are a cornucopia for the sociologist doing research for a *Middletown* on American Liberalism, and for the psychiatrist looking for what I have called his syndrome.

The controversies in which Senator McCarthy was engaged have no relevance whatever to what follows, whose meaning is the same for those who hated, and those who loved McCarthy. It is not necessary to have a commitment to any particular cosmology to enter into a spirited discussion of the political and intellectual controversy touched off by Galileo: unnecessary to believe or disbelieve what Socrates was teaching the youth of Athens, in order to believe or disbelieve that the Court did him justice. I beg the reader who is anti-McCarthy to bear this in mind in the next few pages, during which he will be face to face with the incubus; and I caution the reader who is pro-McCarthy (the liberals can never quite believe such a phenomenon exists) not to lose sight of the ball, which though it may have been thrown by Joe McCarthy, or caught by Eleanor Roosevelt, has nothing to do with the scoring of the game.*

---

* My own views on the McCarthy controversy are elaborately set down in *McCarthy And His Enemies*, co-authored by Mr. L. Brent Bozell (Chicago, Henry Regnery, 1954).

1.

There was Mrs. Roosevelt herself.

Some years ago, after Mrs. Roosevelt had written a column likening McCarthyism to Hitlerism, I suggested on a television program that symbolic of the sluggishness of liberal-directed anti-Communism was the fact that should Eleanor Roosevelt happen upon Senator McCarthy at a cocktail party she would probably refuse to shake hands with him, whereas she would almost as surely shake Vishinsky's hand at the same party. (Andrei Vishinsky was then head of the Soviet delegation in New York.) A day or two later, a reporter brought the remark to her attention. What about it? he asked. Mrs. Roosevelt answered emphatically that she would shake hands with both Vishinsky *and* McCarthy at any future social affair, that in point of fact she once *had* shaken McCarthy's hand (the memory was evidently seared upon her mind); and that, of course, she had seen a great deal of Vishinsky while she was with the UN, hammering out the Declaration of Human Rights.

Still later, in her question and answer column in the *Woman's Home Companion,* the question appeared, "In a recent column you defended your right to shake hands with Mr. Vishinsky, and Senator McCarthy. Would you also have felt it was right to shake hands with Adolf Hitler?" To which Mrs. Roosevelt answered, "In Adolf Hitler's early days I might have considered it, but after he had begun his mass killings I don't think I could have borne it."

I suggest Mrs. Roosevelt's philosophy of hand-shaking does not emerge from the data. If we were to set up a syllogism, here is how it would look:

Proposition A: E. R. will not shake hands with those who are guilty of mass killings.

Proposition B: E. R. will shake hands with Andrei Vishinsky.

Conclusion: Vishinsky is not guilty of mass killings.*

But Vishinsky *was* guilty of mass killings, and surely Mrs. Roosevelt knew that. Indeed, that was a principal revelation of the famous John Dewey Commission of 1939, whose findings on the nature of Stalin's purge trials, at which Vishinsky served as chief prosecutor, settled forever the matter of Vishinsky's blood guilt. What *could* she have been trying to say? That there were differences between Hitler and Vishinsky of the type one takes stock of before extending one's hand? The only explanation Mrs. Roosevelt attempted hangs on the phrase *"after* Hitler had begun his mass killings . . ."— *then* she could not bear to shake his hand. But as mass executioner Vishinsky reached the apex of his career ten years before Mrs. Roosevelt found it bearable to talk with him, and even to work with him, at the United Nations in search of a mutually satisfactory declaration of human rights. (A comparable activity: chatting with Goebbels about a genocide agreement.)

The preceding example is one of any number, easily culled from her column during those years, that demonstrated Mrs. Roosevelt's lack of intellectual rigor. (I grant that following Mrs. Roosevelt in search of irrationality was like following a burning fuse in search of an explosive; one never had to wait very long.) It will be objected that generalizations about the limitations of the

* There is an interesting postscript to my publication of this syllogism several years ago in *Facts Forum News*. Mr. Daniel Bell, a well read editor of *Fortune,* now a professor of sociology at Columbia, wrote me that the syllogism was incorrect, and offered to buy a year's subscription to *National Review,* against my promise to buy a copy of his book (*The New American Right*), if I could get the syllogism certified by a professional philosopher. The syllogism was, of course, duly validated (its structure is that of "denial of the consequent"), and Mr. Bell took out his subscription. I mention this horror story for the benefit of those who cannot bring themselves to believe what I propose to say about the helplessness of the liberal mind when face to face even with elementary logical problems in which ideological Heroes and Villains are involved. P.S. I bought and read Mr. Bell's book anyway. It is a compilation of sociological essays about the social anatomy of American conservatives. It is valuable as a period piece, written at the height of the anti-McCarthy movement.

liberal mind based on anything that she wrote or said are invalid. I disagree, for the reasons I have stressed. The intellectual probity of a person is measured not merely by what comes out of him, but by what he puts up with from others.

What were the voices of dismay, where Mrs. Roosevelt was concerned?

Mrs. Roosevelt was a leading if sentimental mouthpiece of contemporary liberalism, and the fact that she was one of history's truly remarkable women has nothing whatever to do with the fact that she was also a fountain of confusion. In quoting from her I do not pretend to be quoting from a first-ranking liberal scholar or philosopher; but I do ask why first-ranking liberal scholars and philosophers and thoughtful laymen countenanced her on *her* terms (she was a Sage). It may be because a) they were aware that Mrs. Roosevelt's close personal and political association with her husband invested her with a glamor that was highly utilitarian, or because b) (this explanation is both more plausible and more charitable), Mrs. Roosevelt's polemical life was lived right in the heart of the liberal mania, with the result that, themselves bereft of their senses, they were incapable of recognizing that Mrs. Roosevelt was bereft of hers.*

2.

Senator Ralph Flanders, a moralistic Republican from Vermont, rises on the floor of the Senate to ask

---

* Mrs. Roosevelt's book, *India and the Awakening East*, was so unfortunate as to fall into the hands of a non-liberal professional philosopher and logician, Mr. James Burnham, who, evidently, will not soon recover from the experience. "In *India and the Awakening East*," Mr. Burnham opened his celebrated review, "Mrs. Roosevelt was able to complete her flower-strewn march unpricked by the thorns of reason . . ." And concluded: "This furious energy, to which a gigantic ego frantically clings . . . is like a great tank with a drunken driver loose in the crowded streets of a city. It is the onrush of sentiment, unguided and unrestrained by intelligence, reason, or principle. Over whatever subject, problem, plan, or issue Mrs. Roosevelt touches, she spreads a squidlike ink of directionless feeling. All distinctions are blurred, all analysis fouled, and in that murk clear thought is forever impossible."

whether an unnatural sexual relationship among Senator McCarthy's chief counsel, Roy Cohn; Cohn's assistant, David Schine; and Senator McCarthy doesn't satisfactorily explain their bizarre mutual loyalty during the famous feud with the Army. To those unpossessed by mania, this was a smear. Yet in the days immediately following Senator Flanders' address, the publicists worked round the clock to give birth to a new folk hero —the granite-faced, jut-jawed, tough-talking New England dragon-killer. Edward R. Murrow's taut face momentarily relaxed as he contemplated benignly the great moral resources of our democracy. The blasé National Press Club in Washington broke precedent to give Senator Flanders a standing ovation.

One reporter was so prosaic as to press the matter, asking Senator Flanders to crystallize his charges. Are you, he said, saying that these men are perverts? Certainly not, said the Senator; I am merely "asking questions." (Hypothetical situation. A reporter: "Senator, is it true you were paid fifty thousand dollars by the Communist Party to make that speech about Senator McCarthy?" . . . "But *Senator,* I was merely asking questions!")

During an investigation, Senator McCarthy said to General Zwicker of the United States Army, who had proved to be a recalcitrant witness: "Any general who says 'I will protect another general who protected Communists' is not fit to wear that uniform." The liberal community exploded with outrage; had not General Zwicker been decorated for bravery! (Tacit premise: a brave man is automatically fit to wear his country's uniform. Or the alternative premise: No one who has fought bravely in an American uniform could be a pro-Communist. Both premises are of course invalid.) A Senate committee recommended that McCarthy be censured by the entire body for his statement to General Zwicker, and the Senate very nearly did so. When it finally declined (its censure of McCarthy was on other grounds) many liberals cried betrayal, charging the

13

Senate with letting down a man who had fought valiantly for his country.

A month after McCarthy had thus spoken to Zwicker, a member of another congressional committee made challenging remarks, face to face, not to a mere witness, but to a fellow legislator who also had a distinguished background of military service. Congressman B. Carroll Reece of Tennessee had been decorated during the first World War with the Distinguished Service Cross, the Distinguished Service Medal, and the Purple Heart. He had been awarded the Croix de Guerre with palm, cited for bravery by Marshall Petain, by Generals Edward, Hale, and Lewis. Congressman Reece was a legislator of pronouncedly conservative views, and supported Senator McCarthy. His assailant was Congressman Wayne Hays of Ohio, who spoke during a committee hearing over which Reece presided:

Hays: I will say this to [you] . . . that out where I come from we have a saying that if a man double-crosses you once that is his fault: if he double-crosses you twice, that is your fault. I just want you to know you won't get the second opportunity.

Reece: . . . there is no living man [who] can justifiably say that . . . [I] have ever double-crossed anybody or . . . failed to keep . . . [my] word.

Hays: I am saying both . . . is that clear enough? There is no inference there, is there?

Reece: That does not disturb me a particle.

Hays: I know. You are pretty hard to disturb. I thought they had more guts in Tennessee.

No calls for censure, in the *New York Times* or elsewhere, no manifestoes from the Committee for an Effective Congress, no appropriations by the Fund for the Republic; no recorded reprimand, that I ever saw, by any liberal,* even though it was a season of obsession with parliamentary manners.

---

* I did determine, just to see where it would take me, to dog a liberal friend and colleague with whom I was appearing as a panelist on a television program. I decided to stick to the point until he would commit himself on the behavior of Mr. Hays. The best I

Why? Because when Wayne Hays made his remarks, he was engaged in a program of harassment of the Reece committee, and, indeed, succeeded in virtually paralyzing the committee's investigation into the political leanings of the great foundations. In doing so, Hays clearly served the interests of the liberals, who have steadfastly contended that, a) the foundations are not partisan, b) if they are, it is none of Congress's business, therefore c) internal obstructions of a congressional committee's illicit investigations into foundation policy is, by deduction, high patriotic duty. By making the remarks he made to General Zwicker, McCarthy, who had long since triggered the liberal mania, delivered to his opponents potent emotional ammunition. It was made to appear that he was bullying a brave man—in the course of attacking the Army as an institution. Congressman Hays had certainly abused a brave man, and had, by his obstructionist tactics, indirectly attacked an institutional prerogative (the right of Congress to decide what it shall investigate). But he moved in harmony with the Mania.

Was Owen Lattimore a Communist? "Certainly not," one is told by the typical liberal. "The charges against him were dropped by the court, were they not?"

They were. And one repeats, Was Owen Lattimore a Communist? The decision of the Court of Appeals to set aside the indictment of Mr. Lattimore had nothing whatever to do with the question whether, during the period when he directed the policies of the Institute of Pacific Relations, he had worked—as an investigating committee of the Senate put it—as a "conscious, articulate instrument of the Soviet conspiracy." The legal case against Lattimore was dropped on a technicality (the legal difficulty of proving "pro-Communism") which shed no light on the central problem involved. Yet Johns

---

succeeded in getting out of liberal publicist George Hamilton Combs —whose fulminations over the Zwicker incident shattered steel and concrete—was: "Perhaps Mr. Hays' conduct was a little undisciplined."

Hopkins University—and the academic community in general—pounced on the technicality as constituting the exoneration of Lattimore. Academic communities are usually asking that they be allowed to police their own personnel, reminding us that it is *their* business, not that of congressional committees, or vigilante groups, or, worse, "alumni," to decide whether a teacher has abused his profession—but here they joyfully consigned to a court of law the responsibility to decide in their behalf, not merely the *legal* merits of the Lattimore case, over which the Court did have competence, but other questions (over which only Johns Hopkins and Mr. Lattimore's professional peers had competence) as well. I happen to believe that a study of the 13-volume investigation of the Institute of Pacific Relations supports the conclusion of the Senate Subcommittee so conclusively as to render dissent from it (there was none in the Committee—eleven out of eleven Senators concurred) intellectually perverse. But that is not in point; rather the question is whether enough data were assembled to arouse the legitimate curiosity of Mr. Lattimore's colleagues.

I have a copy of a letter from the President's office at M.I.T., addressed to an alumnus who had written in to question the reinstatement, in 1957, of Professor Dirk Struik. Answered Mr. James G. Kelso, Executive Assistant to Dr. Killian, "Upon the dropping of all charges against Professor Dirk Struik by the Commonwealth of Massachusetts, he was restored to teaching duties at the Institute. We are not a legal body with powers of trying or conducting a case. If the authorities cannot find suitable charges, it seems hardly our role to do so."

Now if mathematician Struik, identified by FBI agent Herbert Philbrick as an undercover member of the "professional section of the Communist Party," were to tell his class that the apple didn't fall down on Newton's head, but vice versa; or that the world is flat, or that two times two equals one, the Commonwealth of Massachusetts would be powerless, under Massachusetts law, to act against Mr. Struik. But would M.I.T.? There is not

16

available to the Commonwealth of Massachusetts any mechanism by which to judge whether Professor Struik is a qualified teacher of mathematics; and, let those of us opposed to state control over education hope there never will be. But does this relieve M.I.T. of the responsibility of setting up its *own* standards of professional behavior? The question for M.I.T. is not whether being a concealed Communist is against the laws of Massachusetts, but whether, to qualify to teach at M.I.T., one should meet more fastidious requirements than merely staying out of Massachusetts jails.

But M.I.T. and Johns Hopkins—and liberal leaders of the academic fraternity, whom one might have expected to be startled by the evidence pointing to Mr. Lattimore's and Mr. Struik's abuse of their calling, and resolved to settle for nothing less than an exhaustive examination of the facts, conducted by themselves—allowed, respectively, a court and a legislature to bail them out. In doing so, they slurred over a distinction that one might have expected men of lesser critical faculties to observe; men free of the compulsions of the mania I speak of, which acts to protect from serious criticism any professor who has followed the Communist Party line, particularly if he was caught doing so by a congressional investigating committee.

In like manner, heroes of liberalism are shielded from criticism. Are we not entitled to conclude that the day is close at hand when we will have to agree that Mr. Truman is a great man?

I sat in the spring of 1958 before the television screen and beheld Mr. Truman, with the zest he had for that kind of thing, cavorting from vulgarity to vulgarity, oversimplifying issues, distorting history, questioning motives, provoking base appetites. The restive camera turned from time to time to view the political dignitaries who, stiff in their tuxedos, surrounded the speaker at the annual Jackson Day dinner. I espied Dean Acheson and Adlai Stevenson. I hoped to find them in physical pain. I looked hard. But they did not appear to be suffering. The hauteur and contempt which they knew so well how to display were not aroused even by so raw a provocation. In the spring of 1958, shortly before Mr. Truman was due to sojourn at Yale University, I wrote to a professor there, an old friend and staunch Democrat, whose lot it was to spend hours in close quarters with Mr. Truman. Knowing the professor to be a man of the gentlest personal manner, I wrote asking whether he would not find it hard, ardent a Democrat though he is, to be put up for so long a period with the nation's most conspicuous vulgarian. He replied, gently, that a century ago they were saying exactly that about Abraham Lincoln.

That reply made me realize how profound is the disturbance of which I write. Since receiving it, I have resigned myself to read in history books a generation hence that Mr. Truman, in addition to being a great president, was a remarkable historian (Professor Allan Nevins has said it in as many words): a great master of English prose (Mr. William Hillman, Mr. Truman's ghost writer, has said it in just these words); and the nation's foremost authority on economics (Mr. Truman has said it in just these words).

The failure to take accurate measurements where Mr. Truman is concerned, the failure on the part of men who, however much they approved his personal courage, his decisiveness, his zest, his administration, the political objectives of the Democratic Party—their failure to stand firm in judiciously assessing his dismaying personal limitations leads or would seem to lead to an anarchy in the world of taste and judgment. Let those who worry about deteriorating standards of political discourse worry even more. It is difficult to discourage young demagogues when the record is there that a mere four years went by between the time that President Truman accused Candidate Eisenhower of being anti-Semitic and anti-Catholic, the Republican Party of being inflenced largely by fascists, and the time when Mr. Truman received a doctorate of humane letters, *honoris causa,* from Oxford University.

There was the Reign of Terror. Although those days are well behind us, we should not forget the blood-chilling descriptions of the dissolution of our freedoms at the hands of Senator McCarthy. There is no need to catalogue representative statements about the reign of terror, even the more pathological ones, though I note in passing that Lord Bertrand Russell reported that in McCarthy's America, anyone caught reading Thomas Jefferson was likely to be packed off to jail, and that a professor at UCLA wrote that, in McCarthy's xenophobic America, anyone caught buying a foreign car was likely to be boycotted by members of the American Legion. Perhaps the single most celebrated asseveration was Robert Maynard Hutchins', to the effect that Orthodoxy had closed down American freedom to the point where it had become hazardous to contribute money to Harvard University.*

Finally: In a magazine series describing the Communist attempt to infiltrate our institutions, Dr. J. B. Matthews, veteran anti-Communist researcher, sleuth, and theorist, came to the subject of our churches. He began an article on the Communist attempt to penetrate Protestant Christianity by making a generalization based on statistics: "The largest single group supporting the Communist apparatus in the United States today is composed of Protestant clergymen." This generalization he proceeded to substantiate—whether adequately or not, is not here relevant—in the body of the article itself, where he painstakingly listed the names of dozens upon dozens of the unfortunate clergymen who had collaborated, some knowingly, some not, with the Communist movement, and finally reckoned that, percentagewise, more ministers had been gulled into supporting Communist fronts than teachers or lawyers.

The article in question appeared in a conservative magazine, hence quite a while elapsed before anyone read it. But someone finally did, and lo, at just the mo-

* "Now, after McCarthy's attack on Harvard, they [the foundations] will hesitate to give money to the University." *Look*, March 9, 1954, "Are Our Teachers Afraid to Teach?"

ment when J. B. Matthews was about to be confirmed as the new director of the staff of the Investigating Committee Senator McCarthy headed. In a trice, J. B. Matthews' article was parlayed into "an assault on Christianity!" (Dr. Matthews was an ordained Methodist minister.) A United States Senator said, "When someone makes charges so foul, he ought to have the courage to name names!" (The article was mostly a catalog of names.) Another Senator said, "The naming of so many innocent and godly men in the context of the Communist movement is a morally outrageous act." The liberal press thundered after Matthews' scalp. And so it was given them. Matthews was forced to resign. Without any specific challenge having been made to any of the data on the basis of which the article had been written, or to the celebrated generalization arrived at; without a hearing; without any proceeding whatsoever at which the defendant was given his say. The crisis over, the liberals went back to preaching about the presumption of innocence, fair hearings, and about how one must seek the truth, and endure the consequences.

3.

In America the intellectual elite, within which liberals predominate, a) refused to try to understand the man McCarthy or the phenomenon McCarthyism, and b) acted brutally toward him, and unreasoningly toward it. I do not here explore the reasons why they opposed McCarthy. I am perfectly prepared to assume, for the sake of argument, that the reasons were sound. I am contending merely that the manner in which he was opposed reflected an obsession, and induced the kind of behavior, intellectual and moral, that the liberals do not officially approve of.

Now that McCarthy is no longer in a position to inconvenience them, or prevent them from reading Thomas Jefferson, will the keepers of the American legend go back and look at what really happened? I expect not: the liberals, heeding the warnings of a subconscious solicitude for their self-esteem, will stand their ground. It would be a mortifying journey. They would have to reflect on the data, and the men responsible for the data, which led so renowned a logician as Lord Bertrand Russell to conclude that freedom in America had perished. They would perforce visit a crowded Senate chamber where an elderly and prudish Senator from Vermont dutifully read from a script prepared by an organization composed of many of the nation's mighty,* imputing sexual perversions to Senator McCarthy and members of his staff. They would pause in wonder over the tortured sociological theorizing of scholars who solemnly analyzed the phenomenon of McCarthy's mass support, and concluded ponderously that the only explanation for it was to be found in the geographical and social comings and goings, up and down, eastward and westward, of Catholics and Baptists and rich men and poor men and anti-Ivy Leaguers and traumatized Middle West farmers who couldn't get into Hotchkiss. At least a day would be spent dwelling on the virtual absence of serious literature on McCarthy, and the furious hostility to any dispassionate effort to understand what was going on. And finally, an embarrassed hour with anti-McCarthy confidence man Paul Hughes (see Chapter III) who would tell how he took in and spent, by the thousands of dollars, the money of senior members of the Democratic Party, of Americans for Democratic Action, of the *Washington Post,* by pretending to spy on McCarthy's staff and feeding his employers, day after day, provocative and salacious accounts—all of them completely fabricated—of a day in the iniquitous life of Joseph McCarthy.

Such a journey would be long and humiliating. Not because it would necessarily make one "pro-McCarthy." But because it would shake one's faith in those who

---

* Senator Flanders' speech, it transpired, was prepared by the Committee for an Effective Congress, whose sponsors and officials have included General Telford Taylor, Henry Seidel Canby, Elmer Davis, Oscar Hammerstein II, Prof. Mark de Wolfe Howe, Bishop James A. Pike, Edward Skillin, Michael Straight, Sumner Welles.

framed the case against him. Far easier to continue, doggedly, to insist that McCarthy hounded men whose *only* concern was with free speech; that he labeled *all* his critics pro-Communist; that he was nothing more than a profiteer of the distress of the West. The myths around McCarthy, as recorded by the liberals in the journalism of the past half decade, must not be destroyed, even now that their subject is gone. For the myths have their value. Set up against the facts, they bear evidence to the mania I write of. Senator McCarthy is dead, but the mania he illuminated, in shapes more extreme than ever before thought possible, lives on, and even now asserts control over sensible men whenever their ideology is threatened, questioned, or assessed.

THE DEBATER

I think it is fair to generalize that American liberals are reluctant to co-exist with anyone on their Right. Ours, the liberal credo tells us, is an "open society," the rules of which call for a continuing (*never* terminal) hearing for all ideas. But close observation of the liberal-in-debate gives the impression that he has given conservatism a terminal audience. When a conservative speaks up demandingly, he runs the gravest risk of triggering the liberal mania; and then before you know it, the ideologist of openmindedness and toleration is hurtling toward you, lance cocked.

The tools of controversy are tough, as necessarily they must be. But I wonder when else, in the history of controversy, there has been such consistent intemperance, insularity and irascibility as the custodians of the liberal orthodoxy have shown toward conservatives who question some of the orthodoxy's premises? The liberals' implicit premise is that intercredal dialogues are what one has with Communists, not conservatives, in relationship with whom normal laws of civilized discourse are suspended.

22

Their behavior is anomalous in more ways than one. Not only is it in flat contradiction of the rules of the so-called open society, which of course we don't have, and would have still less if the liberals were in complete charge; it also runs counter to the rhetorical impulses of the day. These are sluggish in the extreme, they place an immoderate emphasis on moderation, and promote a philosophical gentility, deriving from agnosticism, that permeates our moral and intellectual life to its distinct disadvantage.

1.

Let us sample the kind of intemperance I refer to.

1. The letter is addressed, by its author, to his cousin, a gentleman of conservative views who periodically sends around, in mimeographed form, copies of his correspondence with public figures.

> Dear Ken:
> I thought I wrote you once before asking you to take me off the mailing list of your disgusting communication. It does not give me any pleasure to find in my mail a copy of a letter to Senator Jenner, who is so obviously disloyal to everything that America stands for, and a letter, moreover, which so clearly indicates the same kind of disloyalty in its writer.
>
> Sincerely,
> Joseph Alsop

Now several observations suggest themselves, beyond the obvious one that here is a sticky family situation indeed. Why won't Mr. Alsop, a political opponent of the Senator, settle for calling Senator Jenner "mistaken"? Or "stupid"? Or "ignorant"?

But no, he is "disloyal." Disloyal in a sense that officially designated security risks whom Mr. Alsop has vigorously defended, were not.

Let me make my position plain. I do not believe that either John Carter Vincent *or* William E. Jenner ought to be spoken of as disloyal (even in the metaphorical sense in which, let us hasten to assume, Mr. Alsop was using the word in his agitated letter to his cousin). And I know that Mr. Alsop, sober, would agree with me, because he has very often, over the years, expressed his unambiguous contempt for those who use that word lightly. What I should like to know is why he felt free to refer to ex-Senator Jenner as disloyal? Indeed, refer to him as disloyal to *"everything"* America stands for. Would others be excused upon making such statement about, say, George Marshall?

2. From the *Congressional Record* (May 14, 1954). A Senator rises, addresses the chair:

> Mr. President, I wish, for the record, to correct a lie printed in the *Washington Post* of this morning. The lie is carried in the column of the unsavory character called—[let us withhold the name for a moment].

The Senator then went on to quote the statement to which he objected, a statement which spoke of a clandestine political alliance in the Senator's home state. No such alliance existed, the Senator maintained, and continued:

> The writer, of course, knew when he wrote this falsehood that it was false, for he originated it. . . . I should like to suggest to the *Washington Post* that it should not permit its pages to be used for the continuing dissemination of lies manufactured by this man. Furthermore, I think it owes it to its readers to make a thorough investigation of the past record of this man and to publish it, so that all who are subjected to his propaganda may know the character and reliability of its source. . . . It is impossible [to discover] the truth . . . when the pages of the press are permeated with deliberate lies.

Here is a mouthful indeed. No, the speaker is not Senator McCarthy, and the vile offender is not Drew Pearson.

It is Senator William Fulbright, denouncing the late columnist George Sokolsky.*

Now George Sokolsky, a conservative to be sure, was a man of renowned sobriety and courtesy. J. William Fulbright, former Rhodes scholar, former president of the University of Arkansas, is renowned as a leading American liberal, and as the author of a vast skein of international scholarships whose aim is to foster world understanding and tolerance.

George Sokolsky's crime was to infer from events an emergent political coalition—the kind of thing political analysts regularly do, unavoidably running the risk of a misinterpretation. Note Senator Fulbright's call for a) an "investigation" of George Sokolsky (ironic, coming from a man who has so diligently opposed investigations of men and groups which, some people think, pose rather more of a threat than George Sokolsky ever posed); and note how the Senator is b) calling on the *Washington Post* to *fire*—not Drew Pearson, who *does* traffick in political dirt, but who has the good sense to heap it mostly on the heads of men the liberals disapprove of, but a restrained and scholarly commentator on the American scene, and the only conservative columnist, at that period, on the paper. Oh, yes, c) Sokolsky should be suppressed for *moral* reasons—so that we can know the truth.

Book burning? Witch hunting?

3. In the summer of 1958, Mrs. William Knowland reads a pamphlet blasting her husband's political archenemy, Walter Reuther. It is written by Joseph P. Kamp, characterized by the *New York Times* as a "controversial pamphleteer." Mrs. Knowland orders copies of the pamphlet for distribution in California in connection with her husband's campaign against Pat

---

* "CLARE LUCE IS REBUKED BY FULBRIGHT/ For Remarks about Roosevelt, Truman/ Mrs. Clare Booth Luce was rebuked today by Senator J. W. Fulbright (Dem.-Ark.), Chairman of the Senate Foreign Relations Committee, for . . . her use of . . . intemperate language . . . against former Presidents Roosevelt and Truman . . ." Headline and news story, N.Y. *Herald Tribune*, April 16, 1959.

Brown. On learning this, Kamp volunteers to raise money to distribute the pamphlet more widely, in connection with the California political contest. Mrs. Knowland encourages him to go ahead. The *New York Times* breaks a story about the common enterprise of Mrs. Knowland and Joseph Kamp.

Did Mrs. Knowland know, asks a *Times* reporter, that Joe Kamp had once been in jail? No, she did not; she had never, she said, heard of Kamp before. What had been Kamp's offense, she asks? Refusing to give a congressional committee a list of the names of persons who had contributed to an organization Mr. Kamp headed. (Mr. Kamp's legal right to refuse the information was sustained, as the *Times* did *not* mention, when fought out in the related case of *Rumely vs. U.S.* not long after.) Prominent businessmen and politicians were underwriting the distribution of the Kamp pamphlet.

The relevant feature of the controversy is the comment by Walter Reuther on the whole affair. Kamp as pamphleteer is a provocative enemy, Heaven knows. (I repeat: I am not here discussing the merits of the controversies I describe, merely the behavior of prominent liberals caught up in them.) But behold the comment of Mr. Reuther, a man who implicitly speaks from a position of ethical superiority:

"Mr. Joseph Kamp is a convicted hatemonger [Now what is that all about? Mr. Reuther surely knows that there are no laws against "hatemongering," and that in any case, Kamp's conviction had nothing to do with hatemongering*] who went to prison because of his un-American activities [Ah, the precision! And by the way, why is Joe Kamp a villain, and Arthur Miller a hero, for refusing to disclose names to a congressional com-

---

* It has been widely insinuated against Joe Kamp that he is an anti-Semite. Attempting to get to the bottom of the charge at the time the story broke, an editor of *Naional Review* called the offices of the Anti-Defamation League, doyen of anti-Semiticana. An official there, after consulting the files, said the ADL had no data on which to sustain the charge.

mittee?]. I read with considerable interest the sad fact that prominent American industrialists are financing and promoting the efforts of America's most notorious peddler of hate and slander [Read: most offensive to Reuther]. It is most unfortunate that these industrialists have learned nothing from the tragic experience of Fritz Thyssen and other German industrialists who financed Hitler's campaign of hatred."

There you have it: "hatred" "fascism" "un-American" "Hitler"—all funneling into "prominent American industrialists" via Knowland. Just about as complete a smear, right down the line, as one can effect. (Kamp's pamphlet had said about Reuther: "Reuther is smart . . . arrogant . . . shrewd . . . foul-mouthed . . . a vile purveyor of vicious slander . . . ruthless . . . reckless.")

So the intemperance goes, up and down the social and intellectual hierarchy of liberalism. The late professor Mark de Wolfe Howe of Harvard, reviewing the book by Alger Hiss in the *Nation* reflects that "If one has any interest in our national taste it is impossible to refrain from asking how American jurors could be persuaded to give credence to such a man as Chambers in preference to such a man as Hiss. [Chambers, in his own book] . . . tearfully and joyfully exposed himself, [but] . . . sought something more than the indecent satisfaction of undressing in public." Hiss did not follow such a lead, did not allow "his spirit to run naked and weeping through the streets," but rather chose, "proud and thoughtful," to stand "in the ancient ways."* A neat antithesis, for a reviewer who proved too cowardly, in the balance of his review, to assess the evidence on the basis of which it is the settled view of balanced men that Mr. Hiss lied, and lied, and lied. Guarding his dignity and evidencing his thoughtfulness in the ancient ways, he attempted to discredit Chambers by countenancing the vilest insinuations about him and members

---

* We are lucky Professor Howe was not *Censor Librorum* when the *Confessions* of St. Augustine were submitted. He would undoubtedly have sent them back, with a note to take out the emotional bits.

of his family . . . Radio-TV interviewer Mike Wallace, in his column of interviews for the *New York Post*, introduces Randolph Churchill as "an irascible snob." Now for all I know, that is just what Mr. Churchill is; but this is not the way to introduce one's guests, not even obstreperous conservative guests, to one's readers . . . "Senator McCarthy died yesterday in Washington," began the obituary notice in the English Liberal Party's *News Chronicle*. "America was the cleaner by his fall, and is cleaner by his death."

2.

A second marked characteristic of the liberal-in-debate-with-the-conservative is the tacit premise that debate is ridiculous because there is nothing whatever to debate about. Arguments based on fact are especially to be avoided. Many people shrink from arguments over facts because facts are tedious, because they require a formal familiarity with the subject under discussion, and because they can be ideologically dislocative. Many liberals accept their opinions, ideas, and evaluations as others accept revealed truths, and the facts are presumed to conform to the doctrines, as any dutiful fact will; so why discuss the fact?

In dismissing a conservative's contentions, it is not enough merely to say that the matter under "discussion" is closed; it is usually necessary, for the sake of discipline, to berate the person who brought the matter up.

1. Columnist William V. Shannon of the *New York Post,* now an editorial writer for the *New York Times,* reported during the investigation by a Senate Committee in 1958 of the bitter Kohler strike in Kohler, Wisconsin: (my italics) "This is not a controversy where there is plenty of right and wrong on both sides and the disinterested citizens can safely assume the truth lies somewhere between the positions of the two principals. The truth is that the Kohler Company is flagrantly in the wrong. Its position is intellectually *indefensible* and its practices *barbaric*." (The Kohler Company's position,

as stated before the Senate Committee, included a complaint against the United Automobile Workers for committing a recorded 836 acts of violence and vandalism during the strike.) In a word, don't listen to anything Kohler has to say. *Whatever* you do, don't listen.

2. The columnist John Crosby turned critical attention a few years ago to a showing of the now terminated television program, *Author Meets the Critics*. Mr. Crosby was appalled at the performance of the night before, which had featured Admiral Robert A. Theobald, author of *The Final Secret of Pearl Harbor* (Devin-Adair, 1954). Admiral Theobald had been in a position of command during the raid on Pearl Harbor. After the war, he pooled what knowledge he had with what he was able to gather and published a book charging the Roosevelt Administration with gross delinquency and dishonesty in its official accounts of the disaster.

Theobald's charges were—I quote Mr. Crosby— "fantastic . . . The Pearl Harbor attack has been the object of eight separate investigations* . . . which produced literally tons of testimony, evidence and opinion. There are no new facts in the Theobald book—*how could there be?* [Indeed how? If one assumes the correctness of one's position, contradictory data cannot, by definition, exist]—only new and, *according to all reliable historians,* absolutely unwarranted conclusions as to the motives of the President of the United States. [With the stroke of a columnist's pen, three famous scholars, Charles Tansill, Harry Elmer Barnes, and Charles Beard, became unreliable historians.] . . . But what is such a book doing on . . . *Author Meets the Critics?* The program is on the air only once a week and consequently it can take on, at most, only fifty-two books a year . . . You would think that *Author Meets the Critics* would tackle *only those books which a consensus of the critics agreed were the best to come along . . .* " (my italics.)

A consensus of *reliable* critics, needless to say.

---

* Dreyfus was the subject of about as many investigations. Guilty, they all concurred. And then there was the final investigation . . .

My suggestion: Why not have the authors of *un*reliable books come on the program, and burn *them?*

3. In the fall of 1958, Miss Irene Dunne, then a member of the United States delegation to the General Assembly of the United Nations, made a statement to the effect that in her opinion the right to work is a human right. The National Council for Industrial Peace did not lose a minute. It released a statement by Mrs. Roosevelt impugning the motives of all right-to-work proponents. As for Miss Dunne, said Mrs. Roosevelt, she had (my italics) *"perhaps* unwittingly" (That is, quite possibly Miss Dunne *intended to deceive*) allied herself with "those who seek to *enslave* the American worker. The *truth* [as distinguished from that which one hears from such as Irene Dunne] is that the so-called right-to-work proposal does not concern itself . . . with human rights or the right to work . . . Its sole purpose is to enact into law a compulsory open shop that would destroy . . . a democratic right."* In a word, anyone backing right-to-work is deceitful, totalitarian and anti-democratic, or in any case prepared to further the efforts of those who are.

4. When the Chief Justices of the State Supreme Courts severely criticized the federal Supreme Court for its lack of self-restraint (August, 1958) their report was treated as lèse majesté, and indignantly denounced in liberal circles. *New York Times* Supreme Court reporter Anthony Lewis, speaking at Harvard, said of it, "one may recognize the conference report for the exaggerated and political document it is." Professor Alexander Bickel, contributing editor to the *New Republic* and professor of law at Yale University, did probably the best job of verbalizing liberal sentiment: "What business is it of a conference of State Chief Justices to issue manifestoes to the public, and particularly manifestoes criticizing the federal Supreme Court? . . . Assuming

---

* It is to the distinct credit of Mr. Arthur Krock of the *New York Times* that he devoted his column in the *Times,* where criticism of Mrs. Roosevelt was not encouraged, to rebuking Mrs. Roosevelt for her language.

that the Chief Justices had something intellectually coherent to say [here we go: criticism of the Warren Court is intellectually incoherent; as were by implication, the justices and chief justices of the Supreme Court over the preceding 150 years, who reasoned and ruled differently from the Warren Court on identical and related cases], and [we are still assuming] that it was their place to say it, why just now? Why in August 1958? [Why in May 1954, do we decide that segregated schools which have operated side by side with the Fourteenth Amendment for 90 years, are unconstitutional?]"

The bare statement of the Chief Justices of the states was published by David Lawrence, editor of *U.S. News and World Report,* and followed up by a questionnaire directed to members of the federal judiciary soliciting their reaction to it. The *New York Times* undertook to canvass Circuit Court judges to ask their reaction to Mr. Lawrence's communication, and was pleased to report that responses were a blend of "incredulity, indignation, (and) anger." One does not question the unquestionable. Anybody who showed as much respect for the Pope as the typical liberal now shows for Earl Warren, would be considered as a living violation of the separation of church and state.

5. Is Southern opposition to integrated schooling based exclusively on the desire to suppress the Negro? That is what we are consistently being asked to believe. Even so learned and humane a man as the editor of the Jesuits' weekly journal of opinion, *America,* characterized a student demonstration at the University of Alabama against Chief Justice Warren as based on a "passion of race hatred."* There has been more discussion by our thought leaders about the Negro crisis of the past few years than about any other single issue of public concern, and always the suppositions are simply this: that the Southern people desire to freeze the economic, political, and social development of the Negro race, and that this desire alone accounts for their reso-

* The Reverend Thurston Davis, S.J., lecturing at Fordham University, March 21, 1956.

lute opposition to the ruling of the Supreme Court in 1954.

One's instinctive reaction is that if such a charge against the entire white population of the South is so much as thinkable, life in the United States is, as Messrs. Carmichael and Brown suggest, unthinkable. Grant that there are men in the South and elsewhere whose motives are despicable, and that the terms of the crisis are of the kind that encourage a coarse demagogy particularly suited to the temperament of Know Nothingism and the Ku Klux Klan: still, what are we to make of the failure of the opinion makers to distinguish between those whose cant betrays them as racist and demagogic, and those who speak, in measured tones, of the grave constitutional crisis brought on by the Supreme Court's recent passion for imposing its will on the folkways and mores of the nation? Instead of discussion, one hears merely bluster; the fight, we keep on being told, is very simply one between Law and Order, Progress and Reaction, Humanity and Inhumanity, God and Huey Long.

It was not always so. Many of those who now demand blind subservience to the Law of the Land—who refuse to consider the appeals to judicial restraint, even those coming from men of such commanding prestige as, for example, the late Professor Edward Corwin of Princeton, and Justice Learned Hand of the Court of Appeals (dissenters from the tendencies of the Warren Court) —were a bundle of scruples, paralyzed by the finest niceties, when asked to conform to the law of the land in matters pertaining to the national security. Those witnesses who were uncooperative before Congressional committees were widely egged on, in disregard of the law as it was then understood. Albert Einstein urged the intellectual community to refuse to give testimony before Congressional committees looking into Communist penetration. There was, in a word, considerable passive resistance.

How many of these people——whose massive resistance, for example, stopped so-called McCarthyism in its tracks, the massive resistance of whose forebears made the Fugitive Slave Law a dead letter—how many of them are now saying, "I have no sympathy for segregated schooling; but as to the forbidding of it by judicial decree—there are principles involved which we cannot lose sight of . . ."

In 1950, four years before the desegregation ruling, Congress passed the McCarran Anti-Subversive Law which required registration of all organizations dominated by a foreign power. To date not even the Communist Party, let alone any front for the Communist Party, has been required to register under that law —although the McCarran Act's constitutionality was affirmed by the Supreme Court, its enforcement provisions were finally neutralized, on Fifth Amendment grounds. The contrast between the attitude of the Court toward the evasions and foot-dragging of the Communists and the attitude of the same court toward the state governments of the South, is worth noting. Which is the proper way for the Court to act: as it acted in the fall of 1958 toward Arkansas, proclaiming in advance even of the uncrystallized arguments, that *no* circumvention will be deemed legal? Or—as in the case of the Communists—by saying: let us have your objections, one by one; and one by one, we will, judiciously, assess them? Can progress be made if the intellectuals, in their relation to the public affairs of their society, conceive their rights as entitling them to treat an issue with or without regard to its attendant complexities, as they find it ideologically expedient?

6. Mr. Stanley Weigel, of the executive board of the United World Federalists, had this to say concerning American opponents of the United Nations: they are "nationalists—axe grinders, frustrated individuals, inordinate egotists, stifled souls, venomously twisted . . . the spawn of a complex civilization beyond their comprehension . . . They can be cured neither by acts, logic, nor reason. Psychiatrists might help. And the more lawless of them must one day be brought to account before the bar of American justice." Dr. Morris

Zelditch Jr., a sociologist at Columbia University, was quoted (*New York Times,* May 1, 1959) as saying that fluoridation opponents are "largely lower-middle-class Americans disturbed over their rank in society [e.g, D.A.R.?]. They belong to the so-called 'radical right' that tends to support Fascist and neo-Fascist movements and to oppose authority in general." His colleague, Dr. Iago Galdston, a psychiatrist, said merely that the fluoridation opponent is "the sort of person who would strike a match across a no-smoking sign."

3.

Both theoretical and practical challenges are being issued to the liberal. As regards the former, the liberal in controversy has difficulties of a manageable sort: he can always ignore a theoretical challenge. But when the issues take a practical turn, they must, as a matter of obtrusive fact, get some sort of recognition. I mention two. One can refuse to grant intellectual recognition to the conservative contention that the Supreme Court has recently engaged in sociologoical pioneering; but one cannot ignore the fact of deep-South resistance to the segregation decision. One may ignore, ridicule, and otherwise abuse those who maintain it is within the right of Congress to investigate a subversive and conspiratorial attempt to penetrate American institutions; but when the House Committee on Un-American Activities comes to town and actually goes about interrogating flesh-and-blood artists and actors, there is clear and present danger to the liberals' operational control of events, and total rhetoric is accordingly brought to the firing line.

Consider the first: the response to the Southerners' refusal to integrate their schools. To the extent the liberals have influence with the Executive and the Congress, that influence is being used to encourage an indomitable resolution in the teeth of Southern resistance. There to harden this resolution, of course, are the fires of Righteousness. The 14th Amendment to the

Constitution provides that no one shall be denied equal protection under the law (by reason of race, color, or creed). It is a historical fact that separate schooling was not deemed in violation of the Amendment by the men who framed and passed it. Indeed, a number of individual politicians voted both for the 14th Amendment and, in their respective states, for segregated schooling, it never having occurred to them that the two were mutually exclusive. The 1954 ruling brought modern psychological and anthropological skills to the answering of the question: Does separate schooling have the effect of making the Negro feel unequal? The Warren Court ruled (Brown *et al. vs.* Board of Education, 1954) that the evidence is in the affirmative, and that therefore the 14th Amendment has for today broader meaning than once it had.

We are seeing the ascendancy of "inherent meaning" over historical meaning, in matters of law, and with it the moralization of politico-legal issues. Professor Carl A. Auerbach of the University of Wisconsin Law School, who is often seen contributing to the formulation of high civil liberties policy, has raised the point whether the ultimate recourse of the federal government in enforcing compliance does not lie in "The Supreme Court['s holding] . . . that the presuppositions of our democracy require it to take the position that the right to a free, public education is so fundamental a human right that when a state denies this to its children, it deprives them of their 'liberty' without due process of law in violation of the Fourteenth Amendment."* Obviously the development of the theory of inherent meaning has a glorious future ahead of it for those indisposed to dwell on the arid subject of what the law says as written, and what it has been understood to say over the reaches of time.

Another bright thought of Professor Auerbach: If, having failed to devise a means of averting integration through their diverse programs of massive resistance,

---

* "How Congress Can Speed Integration," the *New Leader*, December 22, 1958.

the states decide finally to close the schools, might not the Court hold that "the act of closing the public school [is] itself in contempt of a court order requiring state officials to proceed with integration? Even if it is agreed that nothing in the Constitution requires a state to maintain a public school system, it does not follow that a state may, with impunity, respond to a federal court order to admit Negroes into particular schools by abolishing the public school system."

Here, I contend, we have reached legal sophistry of a clearly totalitarian strain, bespeaking the intensity of ideological passion. What else could bring a professor of law to covet out loud such violent abuses of constitutional tradition? The professor goes unrebuked.

Different people are brought by different forces to their position against segregated schools. Some are moved by pure moral passion, feeling deeply a compassion for all humbled people. Others are not moved by compassion so much as by ideological abstractions about equality. There are certainly men of the first type among liberal interventionists who are seeking to re-order the South; but just as surely, there are, among the agitators, many of the second kind, and it is they, one gets the impression, who are the most militant hectors of the South. What the liberal ideologist in debate generally refuses to reckon with is the political and social problems. In his eyes the problems dissipate at the mere statement of the truism that all men, regardless of color or creed, should be dealt with equally. That abstraction, fiercely loyal though one should be to it, is not, as an abstraction, easily imposed upon an unwilling community, any more than an ordinance to keep holy the Sabbath is easily imposed on a secularist and raucous community. It can be done—by mobilizing tremendous central power. The use of that power to impose an abstract concept *might* have the effect of bringing on at least an external semblance of social equality; but another result is less problematic; it would have the effect of leading us down the road towards omnipotent government. These are problems that loom large in the

36

minds of conservatives, many of whom would unhesi-
tatingly vote for integrated schools in their own neigh-
borhoods, but understand the distinctiveness of the
Southern problem; and, in any case, hesitate to export
their patented solutions to Southern dilemmas. But the
liberal in debate does not honor these demurrers. The
talk is all of how to bring about compliance, and of the
moral necessity that compliance be exacted without
delay. The pitch is struck in an analysis of the Southern
dilemma by Mr. Richard Rovere of the *New Yorker,*
done for the *Spectator* of London in the fall of 1958:

"This story is sworn to by men of good repute. Governor Faubus, who was campaigning for reelection this
summer, addressed a crowd in an Arkansas town and
ranted against the President, the Supreme Court, the
N.A.A.C.P., and just about everything else. When he
had done, a great shaft of light pierced the roof of the
meeting hall, and lo, Jesus Christ appeared. [At this
point one is sure Richard Rovere is pulling our leg, because he would not be a party to the certification of any
supernatural intrusion.] He said that He was the resur-
rection and the life, that those who set man against man
shall not enter the Kingdom of Heaven, that the meek
and the peacemakers are blessed. The mob was quiet
while He spoke; when He finished, there was a great
shout through the hall—'Nigger-lover!' " I wish I had
thought of that!

4.

Another example of the liberal confronted with un-
obliging realities, has to do with the persistent activities
of Congressional committees. Of the thousand and one
protests against the House Committee on Un-American
Activities I have seen, I think the one a few years ago
by Mr. John Crosby, the columnist, most worth relating
in this pastiche of the liberal in controversy.

The proximate cause of Mr. John Crosby's ire one
morning in August of 1954 was the impending visit of
the House Committee on Un-American Activities to
inquire into Communist penetration of the entertain-

ment industry. The Committee and its allies, Mr. Crosby proclaimed, are out "to deprive an actor of his living for something he couldn't possibly know about . . . to hound him for the rest of his life [Tacit premise A: No organization is observably pro-Communist at the time a member joins it. Corollary: After an organization becomes observably pro-Communist, it stops taking members? Tacit premise B: Those who reason otherwise are unjust and vindictive]." Why does the House Committee and its backers want to hound these people? For no better reason than that an actor was once "generous enough to contribute his time and money for Spanish war orphans. [Tacit premise: conservatives can't *stand* generous people, or orphans]." The Committee's arrival in New York was certain to give aid and comfort to the blacklisters, who were urging the industry to boycott performers involved with Communist fronts. And "how do you get on a blacklist? Well, some actors have got on by having foreign names [Tacit premise: blacklisters are reckless, provincial, xenophobic]. Others by having names resembling those of other actors [indiscrimination, again] who once appeared at benefits [Tacit premise: *no* inferences may be drawn from the fact of membership in a pro-Communist organization: a member is almost surely a man of generous impulses] which turned out to be [Tacit premise: It always becomes evident *after* the ball, that the party was in honor of Moscow] under the auspices of Left-Wingers. Blacklisting," Mr. Crosby concludes, "is the shame of a mighty industry . . ." and those who go in for it are "unjust . . . un-American, and . . . pretty close to being criminal."

"Un-American" is not a word Mr. Crosby permits others to use lightly. Certainly not mere Congressional committees.

The central question raised by the Committee on Un-American Activities and the boycott organizations has to do with how a free society can retaliate against those who abuse the popularity they have won as artists. The question is seriously asked by serious persons,

"What should I, as an individual, do, to express my resentment of Paul Robeson's treachery? If Paul Robeson were a politician, the answer would be plain: one would vote against him. But he is a singer. And he brought to his pro-Communist agitation the prestige he acquired as a singer, in part because of my patronage. If it is right that I should fight back against Paul Robeson, where else can I do it other than on Broadway, by boycotting him?"

Or take a case which is less clear-cut—the fellow traveler's. Larry Adler, harmonica player, becomes a sponsor of the Joint Anti-Fascist Refugee League, a Communist front—not because a political organization has any need for the political wisdom of Mr. Adler, but for the obvious reason that Mr. Adler directs the attention of the public to the organization. Did Adler join knowing it was pro-Communist? Or was he duped? If the latter, might he not make the point for the record, before a Congressional committee investigating systematic Communist penetration of the entertainment industry?

Again it does not matter, for the purposes of this investigation, whether one approves or disapproves the Congressional committee, or the boycotters. It matters, however, to recognize that Mr. John Crosby did his best to submerge the relevant issues in a sea of red herrings. The only thing that comes out clearly in his analysis is that entertainers with pro-Communist pasts are admirable men, and their detractors despicable. It is not necessary to rule out the possibility that, as generalizations, both statements might conceivably be made to stand up. But it cannot be contended that Mr. Crosby took a position, and held it responsibly in debate. He just yelled.

5.

I close the chapter with an Orwellian illustration. I refer to a primitive assault on ethical political controversy that went under the name "A Clean Politics Appeal." I reproduce this appeal:

ELMER DAVIS and ARCHIBALD MacLEISH

issue

A CLEAN POLITICS APPEAL

on behalf of:

FRANK CHURCH   RICHARD STENGEL
vs.   vs.
Herman Welker   Everett M. Dirksen

This advertisement was originally run as an experiment—a volunteer citizens' effort to test whether the informed public would actually do something about a situation it had often deplored, whether it would make a genuine effort to balance the flow of special interest money in politics. Thousands of your fellow Americans, responding from every state of the union, have made it a success. We know that you, too, will want to help.

If you are after a special subsidy, tariff or paving contract, don't read any further. We're not your kind of people.

If you are one of the small group of "fat cats" whose contributions will account for 95% of the $200,000,000 that will be spent on politics this year, stop right here. You don't need us to remind you of the importance of this election, or to suggest what you can do about it. The fact is that candidates without access to wealthy supporters or special interest groups are gravely handicapped. Unfortunately, it is often the liberal and more independent candidates who have the least money, particularly in Congressional campaigning. That so many good men win anyhow is an indication of the importance of giving them at least the minimum necessary to make themselves known to the voters who must make the decision.

The outcome of the two contests for which we seek your support will do more to set the tone of national politics in the next two years than any others.

In Idaho, 32 year old Frank Church (D) defeated Glen Taylor for the Democratic nomination and offers Idahoans their first opportunity in a decade to elect a well-balanced and responsible Senator. His opponent in the general election, erratic incumbent Senator Herman Welker, is noted for his pursuit of causes having little relation to Idaho or national interests.

In Illinois, Richard Stengel (D), frequently named by nonpartisan groups as an outstanding member of the Illinois Legislature, has an excellent chance of upsetting incumbent Senator Everett M. Dirksen (R) if he can come even close to matching Dirksen's campaign funds. Dirksen, whom Time Magazine called "the Wizard of Ooze," is one of the most dispensable members of the Senate, and the prospect of his replacement by a young, vigorous and responsible challenger of Stengel's caliber is already attracting impressive Republican and Independent support in Illinois.

The continued success of this experiment—and very possibly the outcome of these elections—is up to *you*. Don't depend on other readers. Make *your* contribution ($100—$5—$3) as large as possible and send it, with the attached coupon, today!

> (signed)
> ELMER DAVIS
> (signed)
> ARCHIBALD MacLEISH

Concerning contributions:
Checks or money orders should be made out to "A Clean Politics Appeal." Contributions may be earmarked; otherwise they will be divided equally between the two candidates. All funds collected from this appeal will go to the candidates. Administration costs are being paid by the National Committee for an Effective Congress.

COUPON:
A Clean Politics Appeal
Box 1163, Washington 13, D.C.
Messrs. Davis & MacLeish:

Enclosed is my contribution of $ . . . . to A Clean Politics Appeal.
  ☐ Please divide it equally between the campaigns of Frank Church and Richard Stengel.
  ☐ Please earmark it as follows:
Name
Address
City and State

In the fall of 1956, this "Clean Politics Appeal" (designed to solicit contributions for the campaign funds of two Democratic candidates for the Senate) appeared as an advertisement in journals and newspapers all over the country. The "administrative cost" of the project was handled by the National Committee for an Effective Congress, a leading organization of American liberals, some of whose members I have already named. The appeal was signed by the late Elmer Davis, and by the poet and professor, Archibald MacLeish. The Appeal, in a word, can be said to have been sponsored by representative American liberals, and highly important ones.

Here were two tireless moralizers who were engaged in moralizing *even while they committed* a grave offense against decent standards of political controversy. Notwithstanding the wide circulation given to the Appeal, I saw not a single protest against it, which confirms once more my thesis that liberals on-the-march, i.e., out to score a point, lose their critical faculties. But let us lead them through their appeal for political cleanliness.

1. In labeling the advertisement "A Clean Politics Appeal" and asking for support of two candidates (Stengel and Church) over their opponents (Dirksen and Welker), the Appeal, in context, implies that the opponents have been guilty of unclean political behavior. No other construction is possible. (One should bear in mind that Mr. MacLeish is a professional writer, as was Mr. Davis; and that both of them had written expressly and sadly about standards of controversy.)

a. Is Senator Everett Dirksen unclean? Does he fight unethically? I am not aware that he does, or even that his opponent Mr. Stengel ever charged him with doing so. It is not relevant that *Time* magazine once called Dirksen oleaginous. The question is, is he unclean? By implication the Appeal says that he is. Where is the proof?

b. What about the late Senator Welker? Did he fight dirty? Is it *unclean* to pursue causes which in the opinion of Messrs. Davis and MacLeish have "little relation to Idaho or national interests"? Certainly the Appeal does not establish that he fought uncleanly. It merely says so—by indirection. I.e., by smear.

2. Mr. Davis and Mr. MacLeish imply that only those who are "after a special subsidy, tariff, or paving contract" would back the two Republicans against the Democrats. No one, it is the gist of the Appeal, could vote for Dirksen and Welker out of a conviction that they would better serve the nation. (Such a thought is presumably unclean.)

3. A "small group of 'fat cats' . . . account for 95% of the $200,000,000 that will be spent on politics this year." Where were those figures assembled? Is a labor union a fat cat? Is labor unionism a special interest?

It is as simple and uncomplicated as this: Messrs. Davis and MacLeish, *et al.,* favored certain programs of social action that Messrs. Stengel and Church also favored. Therefore, Davis and MacLeish, *et al.,* supported them. But rather than solicit help for their candidates by the humdrum expedient of calling attention to their political liberalism, they tone up the contest as involving a fight between Corruption and Integrity, between the general welfare and private greed. That tactic, employed by those who know better, is contemptible.

At the time, I forwarded copies of the advertisement to the then influential Committee for Cultural Freedom, asking its judgment as to whether the Appeal observed the Code on the Ethics of Controversy promulgated by the Committee a few years earlier. My request was met with evasions.

43

Inasmuch as the Committee was composed of some of the most discriminating intellectuals in America, I shrank from the conclusion that, their attention having been forced to the document, they should have failed to smell out what was so reekingly there, namely, polemical foulness. I was therefore relieved to come across evidence that the Committee was distressed by the political venture of fellow members MacLeish and Davis. A letter directed by a dissenting member of the executive committee to its chairman, Mrs. Diana Trilling, stated: "I believe we should clearly say, *as we seem largely to agree,* that the document authored by Messrs. Davis and MacLeish is violative of those canons of ethics we should like to see observed in controversy." It would have been exhilarating to see the Committee spear this violation emanating from the liberal-left; but I suppose that to do such a thing to such a pair as MacLeish and Davis takes the kind of ethical indignation that affiliation with liberal causes tends to dilute; and so one can understand the Committee's reaching, as it finally did, for a technical excuse to avoid direct action.* The point remains that the whole American community was confronted by an arrant breach of the ethics of controversy in the name of clean politics; and no steps were initiated by any liberal to call to the attention of Mr. Davis and Mr. MacLeish the fact that they were riding their mania.

The discussion process in America, between left and right, has come virtually to a halt. That is a great pity, for the reasons that are so often given by liberals themselves, that the ventilation of differing opinions can do much to drain misunderstanding, to make for progress, and harmony.

What is to be done about it? Conservatives feel the Executive is growing too strong, and arrogant, and is not adequately supervised. That is the source of con-

---

* The entire correspondence with the Committee appears in *National Review,* issue of March 23, 1957.

servative misgivings over the secret and apparently hypocritical diplomacy of Franklin Roosevelt before Pearl Harbor. But the charges, whenever they are pressed, are dismissed as "fantastic." They should not even get a public hearing, Mr. John Crosby insists—and scholars, such as Herbert Feis, and Harry Gideonse, and Allen Nevins, say much the same thing. A congressman who wants to know whether there is an observable political bias in the great foundations is denounced virulently everywhere, and branded a "man without guts" by a colleague. Senator McCarthy, who was understood by his responsible supporters to be opposing Executive hegemony in matters of internal security, and challenging the doctrine of the open society which presupposes that a Communist has as many rights as a democrat, before long is spoken of as having outlawed Thomas Jefferson—and is attacked as a homosexual. Herbert Kohler, symbol of resistance to the tidal wave of labor union power, is "intellectually indefensible," while Irene Dunne, who deemed it right that one should be permitted to work without joining a labor union, has joined forces with "those who seek to enslave the American worker." Southern leaders who feel the Constitution has been corrupted by the arbitrary re-interpretation of the Fourteenth Amendment would look on Christ as a "Nigger lover"; and anyway, "what *business*" is it of the justices of the Supreme Courts of the States to criticize the tendencies of the federal Supreme Court? Anyone who believes that the challenge by artists to the cultural, philosophical, and political solidarity of the nation should be answered by a boycott is "unjust," "un-American," and "pretty near to being criminal."

Are these the voices of liberalism? Or are they merely the voices of an aggressive, sectarian liberalism, which in due course will be driven from the Temple? Or is the Temple theirs?

I write about the manners of liberals. Inevitably the question arises, are these manners intrinsic to liberalism?

THE LIBERAL—As Indoctrinator

"SO LONG AS IT'S BLACK . . ."

I HAVE BEEN MAINTAINING for years that American higher education has mostly developed into an engine for the imposition of the prevailing orthodoxy, and that the same people, by and large, who are involved in this operation do not hesitate to instruct the community about the imperatives of academic freedom.

I am sorry to find myself saying this again, because I know from experience that there is not devisable by the ingenuity of man a statement more infuriating than that one. It is offensive to members of the academic community, teachers and students alike, on several counts: The first is the imputed hypocrisy in their doctrinal position. The second is the implication that teachers are agents of an orthodoxy, and students creatures of it, rather than the boldly independent thinkers all of us like to think of ourselves as being. The third relates to the pejorative connotations that cling to the word "indoctrinator"—the result, primarily, of the false antithesis between education and indoctrination cultivated by the liberals themselves.

I say false because education is largely a matter of indoctrination any way you look at it, and because there is no reason to presume unintelligence or shallowness in an "indoctrinator." Socrates was neither unintelligent nor shallow, nor, for that matter, was Adam Smith, or Lenin. But they did not approach a classroom as a vast hippodrome, where all ideas "start even in the race," where the teacher must interfere with none, because the right idea will automatically come romping home ahead of the others. Their method lay rather in exposing the latent disabilities in all but the winning contestant. "The Socratic manner," Max Beerbohm reminded us, "is not a game at which two people can play."

In the hands of a skillful indoctrinator, the average student not only thinks what the indoctrinator wants him to think (assuming there are no prepossessions in the way), but is altogether positive that he has arrived at his position by independent intellectual exertion. That man is outraged by the suggestion that he is flesh-and-blood tribute to the success of his indoctrinators, and gets really sore when you cite his yelps of protest as still *additional* evidence of how good a job was done on him. Yet anyone who turns his attention to it can gather a reliable impression as to the political and intellectual atmosphere in representative American colleges and universities. These institutions are heavily staffed with liberal indoctrinators, and expert ones at that.

But how to accumulate the kind of evidence that makes for a "demonstration"? That is very hard indeed, though it is not hard if one starts the other way around, adducing a young generation of homogeneous political opinion, and asking, How did *this* happen? In imaginative times, the mere emergence of such novels as Mary McCarthy's *The Groves of Academe,* and Randall Jarrell's *Pictures From an Institution,* would seem to serve adequately as demonstration: here, in two novels, is the brilliant—and humorous—last word on the subject of the liberal conformity on the college campus. But in our age Kinsey is prophet, not Eros, and nothing will do but one of those prodigious statistical surveys, to prove that the mountain air is fresh, or the dawn rosy-fingered. Such a work has not been undertaken.*

---

* Professor E. Merrill Root has written a very useful book, *Collectivism on the Campus* (New York, Devin-Adair, 1955) from which many illustrative data can be culled, as has Professor Felix Wittmer (*Conquest of the American Mind,* New York: Meador & Co., 1956).

A few years ago the Intercollegiate Society of Individualists,* a small educational organization that distributes anti-collectivist literature to any student who asks for it, sent out a chatty letter to its subscription list, asking for news of college events. "What, for instance, have your professors been pushing at you?" the letter asked. Had individual professors been preaching redemption by collectivism? "The incidents are important," said the letter cautiously, "not the names. Another thing, please don't get the impression that we want to hear only the bad side. We want a barometer reading. If the situation at your school is encouraging, we want to hear about that too."

Response: "PROFESSORS BLAST GROUP SEARCHING CLASSROOM POLITICS" headlined the Harvard *Crimson* in a four-column fit of indignation. Said the lead, "Four professors denounce as 'ridiculous . . .' 'silly . . .' 'trivial . . .' a right-wing organization's pleas for information about collectivist thinking on the faculty."

Professor Arthur Schlesinger, Jr. told the *Crimson* that "it is characteristic of the state of mind of the country to encourage tattling and snooping." And to give this statement historical depth, as it becomes a professor of history to do, Mr. Schlesinger added: "This illustrates the typical conservative idea that snooping is the way to get personal freedom."

National Review followed up the storm raised by the ISI's innocent little inquiry by addressing its own letter to the editors of college newspapers, proposing a research project into the question whether indoctrination is rife in American higher education notwithstanding the official taboos.

"It is the contention of virtually all educators [the letter read] that it is the business of colleges and universities to 'educate,' not to 'indoctrinate.' By this they tend to mean that teachers should expose students to all points of view adequately and impartially, and should

---

* Now the Intercollegiate Studies Institute.

48

not endeavor to inculcate in them the particular point of view of the teacher, let alone anyone else's views.

"It is the contention of many informed conservatives that a very large number of teachers in this country are in fact engaged in indoctrinating their students in an identifiable position, loosely described as 'liberalism.'

"One can therefore safely assume [I grant this was said ironically] that everyone involved will welcome any intelligent effort to determine whether indoctrination is actually taking place—under the very noses of the anti-indoctrinators; or whether conservatives are unnecessarily alarmed, and the teaching profession vindicated.

"*National Review,* then, solicits evidence of such nature as will clarify the question whether teachers are engaged in indoctrinating their students. For example: Does your economics teacher refer impartially—or in any other way—to the works of Friedrich Hayek, Ludwig von Mises, Lionel Robbins, Frank Knight, W. H. Hutt, Wilhelm Roepke, or to those of any other economist of the non-Keynesian school? Does he take a position on right-to-work legislation? Does your teacher of sociology urge a particular interpretation of man and his behavior, to the exclusion of competing interpretations? If so, by what techniques? Does your teacher of politics insist on or press a particular idea as to the desirable relationship between the Executive and the Legislative? Does your professor of international relations suppress or ignore the writings of learned men who differ with him on how best to cope with world problems? Are they fair in presenting both pro and con views about the United Nations? Do they explore the views of those scholars who believe coexistence with the Soviet Union is impossible? . . . Does the teacher of psychology dismiss religion as fantasy before or after exposing you to the works of St. Thomas Aquinas, or Etienne Gilson, or Reinhold Niebuhr? . . ."

Sample reactions. From *Justice,* of Brandeis University: ". . . the attempt . . . to convince readers of the parallelism between . . . simple spying . . . and a research project is downright infuriating . . ."

From *Cavalier,* of the University of Virginia: "[The project] defies classification . . . [it is] in one sense the work of someone having Fascist leanings, and most generally, that of a 'crackpot.'" From the *Spectator,* of Columbia University: ". . . we don't know whether to laugh at, or be just plain revolted by [the project]. It is the most outrageous attempt to instigate snooping and sneaking and arouse suspicion in the classroom, that we have heard of [herewith a classic compliance with the Doctrine of Understatement] in quite a while." And from the *Arrow,* of Hunter College: ". . . Judas only received thirty pieces of silver. We can all work our way through college turning in teachers with whom we disagree. More fun than a Ku Klux Klan meeting . . . What sort of proponent of academic freedom can Mr. Buckley be, when he advocates a system that by its very nature breeds suspicion, conformity, fear, animosity, distrust, and thoughtfulness?" (Yes, "thoughtfulness.")

There we are. Teachers, with the ardent support of their students, tend to ask for their classrooms the kind of privacy they might be expected to ask only for a connubial couch. They will not, in a word, cooperate in a research project whose findings might serve to demonstrate the enormous gap between theory and practice. That is why a report on ideological indoctrination in American colleges must perforce be impressionistic and microcosmic, as this one will be.

1.

It is curious that at a time when the art of indoctrination has become for urgent political reasons an advanced field of study, acquiring a considerable body of knowledge of its own, we continue to think of indoctrination in caricature. The indoctrinator of the public image is the teacher with hickory rod in hand who says to a classroom of frightened students, "Now repeat after me: *The movement to lower the tariff*

barrier is a movement to destroy our standard of living."
It was never really so, and certainly is not so today.

I believe firmly, as I have hinted above, that most professors are to some extent indoctrinators, and that those who are not to any extent indoctrinators, should be. Every morally active man must come to conclusions. He does not rule out the possibility of modifying, or replacing those conclusions later; but they do not, for that reason, bind him any the less at any given moment. And if they are conclusions that fire him intellectually and passionately (and all conclusions by men of energetic heart and mind should be of that kind), he should be expected to impart them to his students.

The relevant question is not so much, "how many indoctrinators are there in the big name American colleges," as 1) what is it they are inculcating; and 2) what techniques do they, as indoctrinators, use?

As to the first question, they certainly inculcate liberalism. The root assumptions of contemporary liberalism I attempt to dig out in a later chapter (see VI). For present purposes suffice it to bear in mind the component parts quoted above in the letter to the college editors. Specifically: the typical economics department makes little or no use of the dissenting works of Hayek, von Mises, Robbins, Hazlitt, Knight, Hutt, Roepke, *et al.* The approach of Lord Keynes is established doctrine. As a general rule, professors of economics oppose restrictive labor legislation, including right-to-work laws. Their position on right-to-work, like their position on many other public issues, is traceable less to professional or theoretical imperatives that grow out of their economic *Weltanschauung,* than to the demands of political alliances that bind so strongly the academic community, and organized labor, to the Democratic Party. The sociology departments are secularist, positivist, and materialist. The single serious competing view of man and his behavior is essentially spiritual. That view does not tend to get a serious hearing, even though religion and the "science" of sociology are not, by all respectable sociologists, posited as mutually exclusive. The departments of political science tend to urge the view of a dominant executive, tend to disparage states' rights, to argue the need for the centralization of power; and do so, moreover, without a serious canvass of alternative views, except perhaps as curiosities. The international relations department is heavily neutralist, highly ideological on the subject of foreign aid and the United Nations; it does not pause thoughtfully over literature that a) questions the feasibility of co-existence, b) is critical of doctrinaire foreign aid, and c) rejects the charismatic view of the United Nations. The departments of psychology are forthrightly secularist.

I grant that I have merely affirmed a situation to be as it is, and have not "proved" that it is so. I have mentioned some of the difficulties that stand in the way of systematic exposure. But even when evidence of the most concrete nature is adduced, as I adduced it in a microscopic study of the ideological impact of higher education (in *God and Man at Yale*), it does not sway the mind unwilling to dislodge its presuppositions. In affirming these facts, then, I shall simply have to say: They are correct, and as visible to anyone who looks into the matter as they are to me. They will not be denied by a dispassionate observer of the academic scene.

2.

Of more immediate interest than the conventional revelation that liberalism is the diet of the average undergraduate, are the techniques of indoctrination. Specifically I am interested in the approaches to conservative dissent. I think they fall into three general categories. They are 1) Conservatism does not exist. 2) Conservatism does exist, but it is not an intellectual problem; it is one of pathology. 3) Conservatism does exist—as a lowering political force that threatens to ring in a new Dark Age.

A top exponent of the first academic approach to conservatism is Professor Louis Hartz of Harvard, the author of *The Liberal Tradition in America.** His conclusions are both historical and philosophical. There never was a sure-enough conservatism in America, he maintains,** the American experience having been dynamic, revolutionary, pragmatic, kinetic. What is sometimes mistaken for conservatism is an ad hoc agglomeration of forces, brought together temporarily by a proximate common interest. Conservative dissent then (one deduces), whether in economics, in politics, in sociology, in philosophy, or in psychology, can be assumed to originate from a material source, and can be ignored except as it succeeds in being embodied in a politically presumptuous movement, in which case: Overcome it.

The second general approach is based on a thesis that is both more serious and more frivolous. It is serious because it has captured the attention of serious men; it is frivolous because what it asserts is preposterous. I refer to the cult of *The Authoritarian Personality*.

The book in question was published in 1950, the flower of a grandiose research project sponsored by the American Jewish Committee, in which the Institute for Social Research, the Rosenberg Foundation, the University of California, and Western Reserve University had a hand. The idea was to track down the causes for the unaccountable persistence of widespread conservative sentiment in America. The book, written by a staff headed by T. W. Adorno, has much conditioned the liberal attitude toward conservative dissent.

If one dismisses *a priori* the possibility that there are rational grounds for resisting the liberal view of things, one necessarily looks elsewhere than to reason for explanations of such discomfiting phenomena as, e.g., the great popularity of the late Robert Taft. Mr. T. W. Adorno did just that, of course, and came up with

---

* Harcourt Brace, 1955.
** There are conservatives to be found maintaining the same thing. Mr. Ralph de Toledano has a brilliant and persuasive chapter in *Lament for a Generation* (Farrar, Straus & Cudahy, 1959), making this point.

what he was looking for after completing a massive research project that marshalled the very latest expertise in depth-interviewing. Adorno's techniques, we may note in passing, are questioned even by colleagues generally sympathetic to his thesis. For example, sociologist Margaret Mead, criticizing an article by Professor Richard Hofstadter which leans heavily on *The Authoritarian Personality*, decries his "parochial explanations," as based on "the psychoanalytically oriented, German-modeled, authoritarian personality study, in which the character structure of lower-middle class Americans is equated, [disregarding] cultural differences, with the character of lower-middle class Germans as prone to victimize the weak . . . There might be no atom bomb [to account for McCarthy's popularity], no hydrogen bomb, no explicit insistence on a polarized world, no Communist China to alter the attitudes of the American people." Indeed an entire compilation of *Studies in the Scope and Method of 'The Authoritarian Personality'* * is given over to devastating (though highly respectful) analysis of almost every aspect of the project's methodology.

But that is to break a butterfly on a wheel, surely; one needs no advanced degrees in clinical psychology and psychoanalytical theory in order to penetrate the fallacy of *The Authoritarian Personality*. Its thesis is very simply this: American conservatives (primarily members of the lower middle class) are the way they are politically because of marked tendencies to authoritarianism. The authors of the project *began* with the assumption that anyone who is opposed to the federalized welfare state is likely to be "unenlightened" in his attitudes toward science and religion; that such persons tend to accept the authority of an organic moral order, to hate Jews and Negroes, to entertain an unconscious desire to grind their heels in the faces of the weak. These postulates are fed into a mill, mixed with

---

* Edited by Richard Christie and Marie Jahoda, The Free Press, Glencoe, Illinois, 1954.

projective questionnaires and clinical interviews, seasoned with the intercorrelation of the interviewees' "PEC" (political and economic conservatism) scale, their "AS" (anti-Semitism) scale, their "E" ethnocentrism) scale, and their "F" (implicit pre-fascistic tendencies) scale—to produce the stereotype: "the authoritarian personality."

My own view is that the generalizations, where they are not groundless, are meaningless; that to the extent they say a conservative is something else than what he is, they are wrong,* and to the extent they prove a conservative is a conservative, they are supererogatory. But I am not here to argue with Mr. Adorno; merely to state that he has had influence, and has disciples **; and that his thesis is marvelously convenient for those who refused to concede that there are rational grounds for conservative dissent from the liberal orthodoxy, but were hard pressed, until relatively recently, to point to other grounds.

3.

There is the third approach (it does not conflict with the second), which presupposes a powerful conservative movement-on-the-march, against whose aggressions it is the tacit responsibility of cultured and educated men to unite. This approach, in addition to being very flexible, sustains the indispensable impression that the academic community, in the process of cultivating a

---

* And logically circular, ergo fraudulent. E.g., from the studies compiled by Richard Christie and Marie Jahoda, ". . . a major finding of *The Authoritarian Personality*—the demonstration of a syndrome of attitudes of political conservatism and authoritarianism, as revealed by the formal statistics of a correlation between the numerical scores—could instead reflect the mere fact that the PEC scale and the F scale both contain questions which are basically similar in content."

** One or two other works in this genre: "Conservatism and Personality," by Herbert McCloskey, American Political Science Review, March, 1958; *The Academic Mind: Social Scientists in a Time of Crisis,* by Paul Lazarsfeld, Wagner Thielens, Jr., Glencoe, Ill., The Free Press, 1958.

conformity, is doing so in the cause of nonconformity—vis-à-vis the world at large.

I touch on a substantial difficulty of the liberal indoctrinator. The canon of academic freedom is very clear: no one idea is to find corporate favor in educational institutions over another; clear, too, are the ringing declarations of the open society, which stress the need for a respectful attention to dissenting views. It becomes necessary under the circumstances for the indoctrinator to give the impression that tolerance and openmindedness *are* being exercised; that the student is making his decisions independently of external pressure, suasion, or even leadership; and that the academic community is an embattled little enclave, deep in the heart of Philistia; so that what may appear to the resident of that enclave to be a conformity of opinion is, macrocosmically, a giddy nonconformity.

As I indicated in the previous chapter, it is not easy to tell whether a) the liberal really believes that two sides of an issue are being heard; b) is blind to reality; or c) is indulging in a little hypocrisy—driven to it, he might rationalize to himself, by some manifest impracticalities in the doctrine of academic freedom which are best not brought out into the open. ("Are you *really* supposed to treat all ideas as equal? Fascism, for example, are we to be neutral about *it*?") What alternatives does the liberal in fact present to the student? I mean, what alternatives to the Right of liberalism? A brilliant recent expression of the liberals' idea of alternatives, though political in formulation, I bring up in this section on academic matters because it is quintessentially liberal, and betrays an attitude that governs alike in academic and political matters.

From *Meet the Press,* December 18, 1955. The guest is Mr. Joseph L. Rauh, Jr., President of Americans for Democratic Action.

Question: Mr. Rauh, the ADA supports the Democratic Party, endorses it, most of your leaders are members of the Democratic Party; why then do you keep up the pretense that you're independent and non-partisan?

Rauh: We *are* independent and non-partisan, Mr. Spivak. We look for Republicans to support. We did support in the last election Senator [Clifford] Case—along with, I must say, a vice chairman of the ADA, [the Democrat] who was running against him. We used to support Senator Morse when he was a Republican, but he did us a dirty trick and became a Democrat.

Q: Are you saying then, a Republican has to be a Democrat for you to support him?

Rauh: No, he has to be a liberal . . . We would love elections in which both candidates are liberals. That's a luxury we don't get enough of.

Q: . . . Mr. Rauh, which of the Democratic candidates, Adlai Stevenson or Governor Averell Harriman, or Senator Estes Kefauver is ADA going to support?

Rauh: . . . I really don't have any judgment between the three of them, I think they're all fine liberal candidates.

Q: Since you're an organization dedicated to making the Democratic Party more liberal, which of the three do you think *is* more liberal?

Rauh: We're organized to make *both* parties more liberal . . .

Q: Would you like to see Chief Justice Warren nominated on the Republican ticket? Would you support him?

Rauh: I think it would be a great luxury for the American people to have Chief Justice Warren on the Republican ticket and have such men as Harriman, Stevenson, or Kefauver on the Democratic ticket: then we can't lose whatever happens.

Q: What would the ADA do, do you think?

Rauh: . . . I don't feel I can say what we'd do in a Warren-Stevenson race, for example, except to call "Thank goodness there was such a wonderful choice [sic] of candidates."

That is the kind of choice the student at the typical college enjoys full freedom to make. The choice of candidates. But not of platforms. The conformity I write of is not one that precludes choice, but sets the limits within which the choice may be made. (I remember in the summer of 1952 hearing it said to an informal audience, by one of the serene-type college officials who are born to assuage the fears of fretful alumni, "Tell me now, do you *really* think the boys are so radical, when they voted 70 *per cent* for Eisenhower in the undergraduate preference poll a couple of months ago?" It worked wonders. Unreported finding of the same spring poll: Senator Robert A. Taft won *five* per cent of the *Republican* vote. The significant political contest in 1952 was between Taft and Eisenhower, over the question whether the Republican Party should go Right or Left. The students did not reveal themselves as having been confused by their teachers as to which it should be.)

The second requirement, as I say, is that the student should have the impression that he is making up his own mind. In point of fact, very few people make up their own minds intellectually, for which we have Heaven and all the saints to thank. "Lean not on thine own understanding" is a Biblical injunction, and there is no mischief maker quite like the person who assumes himself a totally autonomous intellectual and moral being and proceeds to inflict himself upon his fellow men. We stand, as Mr. Russell Kirk never tires of reminding us, on the shoulders of giants, and the moment we dispense with their support, we come crashing down to earth, where we live intellectual and moral lives circumscribed by drastically foreshortened horizons.

I do not, in short, myself believe it is in the least bit undignified to confess to having been critically influenced in one's thinking by a teacher, or a faculty, or a book; but the accent these days is so strong on atomistic intellectual independence that to suggest such a thing is, as I have noted, highly inflammatory. There is literally no way to prove, other than by appealing to the self-evident, the influence of a faculty on a student's opinions; but I record, for what it is worth, an earthy example, not without significance.

In the fall of 1952, the Harvard undergraduate paper, the *Crimson,* conducted among its readers a simple poll, asking merely which presidential candidate, Stevenson or Eisenhower, was favored. The freshman class (which at the time had spent only about five weeks at Harvard) voted Republican 3-2. Upper-classmen, by contrast, voted Democratic 5-4. Graduate students voted Democratic 2-1. The graduate faculty of Harvard voted Democratic 4-1.

At Yale University, at about the same time, polls asking the same question revealed a bitter political division among the faculty of the Law School, where the vote was Democratic by 14–1. At the Divinity School (another civil war), it was Democratic by 13-2. Let the person who wants to wrestle with these statistics blurt forth his secret belief that there is a correlation between "level of education" and "political liberalism." But if I may, I shall put it my own way: there is a correlation between the length of time one spends studying at the feet of liberals and the extent to which one comes to share their views. That is to say, large scale indoctrination goes forward—as one would expect—in our colleges and universities.

Again: Dr. Philip E. Jacob, in his treatise on *Changing Values in College* (Harper, 1957), described the difference between the Vassar senior, beneficiary of four years of Vassar education, and the Vassar freshman:

> The senior more often than the freshman justifies the breaking of rules on occasion, including civil disobedience; questions whether "communism is the most hateful thing in the world today," or whether the American way of life should be preserved unchanged; would prefer to betray country rather than best friend.
>
> The senior goes to church and prays less than the freshman, and is less likely to believe in . . . a life hereafter, and even that there is a God.

59

The senior is more likely than the freshman to admit to conduct and attitudes contrary to conventional moral taboos concerning drinking, telling the truth, sexual propriety and even theft. She feels people would be happier if sex experience before marriage were taken for granted in both men and women . . . She thinks she would probably get into a movie without paying if sure she would not be seen.*

Senator (then Mayor) Joseph Clark wrote in the *Atlantic Monthly* **: "How can the leadership problem be solved [to bring about a liberal rally]? Essentially it is a matter of recruitment. Fortunately, free compulsory education works for the liberals. With the enormous increase in the number of high school graduates, there is a greater awareness of political problems and of the need for political action than ever before. There is a wider understanding of the basic fact that democracy is social and economic as well as political."

Senator Clark means he's glad the schools tend to indoctrinate the students with his views.

The illusion of nonconformity was greatly helped along during the McCarthy years, when prominent academic spokesmen ventured hysterical opinions about the death of freedom in the outside world, and its imminent extirpation in the academic community; as, for example, Robert Hutchins' aforementioned article questioning whether money could safely be given to Harvard University, and Bertrand Russell's doubting whether it were any longer safe to read the works of

---

* Dr. Jacob's findings confirm those of novelist-critic Mary McCarthy, published in *Holiday* (May 1951): "A wistful respect for the unorthodox is ingrained in the Vassar mentality . . . The effect of this training is to make the Vassar student, by the time she has reached her junior year, look back upon her freshman self with pity and amazement. When you talk to her about her life in college, you will find that she sees it as a series of before and after snapshots: 'When I came to Vassar, I thought like Mother and Daddy. I was conservative in my politics.' . . . With few exceptions the trend (i.e., the indoctrinational impulse—WFB) is from the conservative to the liberal, from the orthodox to the heterodox."
** "Can the Liberals Rally," July 1953, pp. 27–31.

Thomas Jefferson. Such heady talk persuades the student that the way to nonconformity is—conformity with the precepts of his own intellectual group; which is dominated by liberalism.

4.

Let those who find it hard to believe that indoctrination and the suppression, by one or another technique, of conflicting conservative opinion go forward in our colleges and universities consider the following episode. If such a thing could have taken place, in the normal course of events, it becomes easier to believe that indoctrination camouflaged by the techniques I mentioned can be taking place widely.

Professor Fred B. Millett is not only head of the English Department of Wesleyan University but former President of the American Association of University Professors, the leading professional lobby for academic freedom. Professor Millett is in the habit of sending out a newsletter, *FBM's Newsletter,* to fellow professors. A few years ago, FBM wrote proudly on how he had disposed of charges that left-wing ideology was debasing literature, charges made by Professor E. Merrill Root, a distinguished poet and critic, formerly Professor of Literature at Earlham College, in an essay published by the conservative Washington publication, *Human Events.* Wrote Professor Millett, in his newsletter:

In English 48 (Literary Criticism), my most interesting experience came from having the students in an hour-written [i.e. examination] point out the fallacies—with reference to the nature of literature, the process of criticism, and the relation between literature and life—in one of E. Merrill Root's essays, "The Culture of the Left," which appeared in a sinister little American-Fascist publication *Current Events* (sic) . . . My students, I may say, did a beautiful job of exposing the unsound assumptions of this preposterous performance.

61

I bet his students did, all right, and if they called Mr. Root a fascist-by-association, they might well have earned a reward for showing a high critical acumen, which one could expect them to show, sitting at the feet of FBM; who, undoubtedly, has also impressed upon his students, as he impressed upon so many others during his tenure as President of the American Association of University Professors, that one compelling reason for academic freedom is that students are permitted to make up their *own* minds about things, rather than submit passively to indoctrination. A sinister thing, indoctrination, advocated only by American Fascists.

THE LIBERAL—In Action

THE TESTAMENT OF PAUL H. HUGHES

> *Let us do away with confidential informants, dossiers,*
> *political spies . . . No one can guess where this process*
> *of informing will end.*
>
> JOSEPH L. RAUH, JR., in
> *The Progressive,* May 1950

CERTAINLY JOSEPH RAUH would never have guessed that his own use of confidential informants, dossiers, and political spies would one day result in a jury of his peers' refusing to take his word over that of a self-confessed liar and confidence man.

From time to time in the course of events a symbolic incident suddenly plants before our vision the concentrated meaning of a complex historical process. Though humbler in scale and more banal than the mighty exemplars that we find in history books, the trial of Paul Hughes was such an incident. Paul Hughes was a minor scoundrel. But he dealt with major figures on the American scene, and in the nature of his dealing with them lies the key to major contemporary enigmas.

The witnesses who appeared in the trial of Paul Hughes are the responsible leaders of powerful institutions that are at the ideological core of contemporary liberalism. They included Joseph L. Rauh, Jr., at the time Chairman of Americans for Democratic Action, and the most conspicuous and active civil rights lawyer on the American scene. Telford Taylor, prominent civil rights lawyer, sometime chairman of the National Committee for an Effective Congress—a forceful liberal lobby of lustrous membership. The late Philip Graham, James Russell Wiggins, and Alfred Friendly, the three top officials of the *Washington Post and Times Herald,* a leading organ of American liberalism. James Wechsler, co-founder of Americans for Democratic Action, editor of the *New York Post.* General Cornelius Mara, White House aide and intimate of President Truman. Clayton Fritchey, editor of the Democratic Party's official magazine, *Democratic Digest,* and deputy chairman of the Party's National Committee. Also involved in the Hughes case, though not as witnesses, were Robert Eichholtz, Washington attorney, Rome representative of the Marshall Plan under the Truman Administration, and generous financial contributor to the ADA; Paul Porter, former high official of the Roosevelt and Truman administrations, and former publicity director of the Democratic National Committee; Clark Clifford, special counsel and leading advisor to President Truman (1946–1950).

Here was in no sense a casual selection of unrelated individuals. The evidence shows that they and their institutions are actively interrelated—"interlocked," as one says of business corporations. These men know each other intimately, confide in each other, collaborate actively, give each other mutual support and assistance. It was they who were, historically and philosophically speaking, up for judgment at the trial of 35-year-old half-literate confidence man, Paul Hughes.

1.

Consider the story.

In January 1954, Paul Hughes, recently discharged from the Air Force, was still without a regular job. Immediately after his discharge the previous summer, he had approached the staff director of Senator McCarthy's Subcommittee on Investigations—with a lurid tale of high treason at the critical American Air Force base at Dhahran, where he had recently been stationed.

McCarthy aide Francis Carr took notes, checked the story (as it was his duty to do), arrived at the conclusion in a matter of days that it was all a fabrication, and refused further association with Hughes, whom he never saw again. Hughes tried the FBI. Again his story was checked; again he was shown the door. Paul Hughes crossed the street.

He called on retired General Mara, friend of Harry Truman and big Democrats who, after a few sessions with Hughes, put him on, enthusiastically, to Clayton Fritchey, editor of the *Democratic Digest*. He was a secret member of the staff of Senator McCarthy's committee, Hughes lied to them, and was disgusted by what he saw going on about him. He was prepared, *pro bono publico,* to report secretly to them the secret doings of the Committee. They signed him up zestfully, dutifully accepted the aliases he imposed on them ("Yale" and "Ewing"), and paid him, over a period of a few months, $2,300 for "expenses." In January, evidently seeking to broaden his clientele, Hughes approached the worldly Joseph L. Rauh, Jr. Before he was through with him, he had $8,500 of Rauh's money.

Hughes unfolded to Rauh a phantasmagoria of treacherous doings on the part of McCarthy and his associates—so grotesque and bizarre, so beyond the normal imagination, that they would surely have struck Rauh as incredible had they been imputed to a Communist, rather than to Senator McCarthy. But Rauh was instantly taken in, and asked Hughes for more and more and more, so hot was his lust for anti-McCarthyana.

Hughes obligingly brought in a 94-page document which is, in its way, a work of genius. One might easily suppose, on reading it, that it was the work of a master psychiatrist seeking, simultaneously, to assuage and to aggravate a patient of unbalanced political outlook. The salve was there—for here was confirmation in abundance of the worst one could imagine about McCarthy; and also the galvanizer—here was a call to glory, a call for extraordinary exertions to destroy the monster McCarthy.

There was something in this remarkable document that fed on, and then quickly nourished, every liberal political neurosis of early 1954. Here was evidence of a secret and dark alliance between Eisenhower and McCarthy; of tantalizing rivalries between the staffs of the Jenner (Internal Security) and the McCarthy (Government Operations Investigations) committees; of imminent plans to enter into forbidden communication with Igor Gouzenko, the inaccessible defector who blew the Soviet spy ring in Ottawa and was still being kept under wraps, nine years later, by the Canadian Government; of marital problems developing between Senator and Mrs. McCarthy; of a clandestine White House conference at which a smear campaign against the Democratic Party was programmed; of McCarthy's personal views (revealed through a transcription of miscellaneous animadversions) on such disparate persons and things as Attorney General Herbert Brownell, Air Force bases, Drew Pearson, ethics, Leonard Hall; of McCarthy informers scattered about in the White House, in the Central Intelligence Agency, in the State Department; excruciating teasers about informants whose identity had not been disclosed; and the whole wrapped up in a chaotic package of notes, official memoranda, inter-office communications, secret transcripts, here virtually illiterate, here eloquent, always steaming with drama, and emitting a sex appeal irresistible to professional anti-McCarthyites.

Thus the nine-months-long association had begun. Now, two years after the fateful encounter, Joseph L. Rauh, Jr. sat in a federal courtroom in New York, at the trial, for perjury, of Paul H. Hughes. It transpired that after leaving Rauh, *et al.,* Hughes (in a maneuver too complex to go into here) had, while posing as a private investigator, informed a grand jury investigating the redefection of Harvey Matusow to Communism, that Joseph Rauh and his associates had been instrumental in persuading Matusow to disavow the sworn evidence he had given in previous years against his sometime associates in the Communist Party. (Rauh *et al.* denied any foreknowledge of Matusow's about-face.) The grand jury, in exploring Hughes' charge, had unearthed the story of his dealings with Rauh, and indicted him for perjury in the Matusow matter. A second charge against Hughes was that he had perjured himself in telling the grand jury that Rauh had associated with him knowing all along the fraudulence of his representations.

Rauh sat down on the witness chair with the unenviable task of persuading the jury that, though a sophisticated and experienced man of the world, he had worked hand in glove with Hughes without ever suspecting him of being a phony. Hughes' court-appointed defense attorney took on the obligation of attempting to persuade the jury that this was unthinkable; so the legal battle went forward between two competing points of view, 1) that Rauh was a knave (argued by Hughes and his lawyer), and 2) that he was a fool (argued by Rauh and the government).

Rauh told the jury that he had been interested only in developing a legal case against McCarthy, not in having a prurient view of McCarthy's affairs. In that case, why did he not instruct Hughes to limit his reports to evidence of legal wrongdoing? Rauh began to hedge.

Q: Wasn't it your testimony, Mr. Rauh, [Hughes' lawyer asked] that the sole thing you were interested in with reference to Senator McCarthy was evidence of the illegal acts; and any other type of information, no matter how derogatory about Senator McCarthy, you were not interested in at all?

Rauh: . . . I said what I was interested in was illegal and unlawful acts. I don't remember whether I ever specifically said [to Hughes], "No matter how derogatory it is, please don't furnish it." That might go a little bit farther than [interrupted].

Alfred Friendly of the *Post* (alias "Dinwiddie") had an equally difficult time explaining why he had jotted down—in longhand—page after page of idle anti-

McCarthyana after talking with Hughes,* which had nothing to do with allegedly illegal activities. Clayton Fritchey more or less gave up the attempt to persuade the court that his interest in McCarthy's affairs was limited. Why was he so interested, he was asked, in the fact that, according to Hughes, McCarthy had a sympathizer on the *Louisville Courier-Journal,* in violation of no known or conceivable law? "What did *that* have to do with illegal activities?" the judge asked. "It happened —a friend of mine happened to be publisher of the *Courier-Journal* . . .", was the answer.

The Court wanted to know why, if Hughes' employers were exclusively interested in McCarthy's alleged illegalities, they had not turned the whole matter over to the Justice Department, rather than keep it within the bosom of the National Committee for an Effective Congress, the ADA, the *Washington Post,* and other factional instruments of a political movement. Several witnesses had a go at answering the question. "Did you explain to Mr. Hughes why you called in Mr. Fritchey and, let's say, not Mr. Brownell?", General Mara was asked. "I don't quite—well," said the General, "the only reason I called in Mr. Fritchey was, I felt he had newspaper background, that he could analyze this thing . . ."

> Attorney for the Defense. [Rauh had just admitted that Hughes informed him that McCarthy's spy on the *New York Post* was the *Post's* cooking editor]: Did you call Mr. Wechsler, editor of the *Post,* and tell him?
>
> Rauh. Yes, sir.
>
> Q. You didn't feel that the cooking editor was going to slant any recipes in McCarthy's favor, did you?
>
> A. That wasn't the purpose. That wouldn't have been the purpose to have somebody there.
>
> Q. What *was* the purpose of McCarthy having a spy as the cooking editor?
>
> A. Because a cooking editor like anybody else has access to all the records, files and clips and other

---

* Court Exhibits 52A through 52D.

matters on the paper and to all the discussion. It doesn't matter who the person is. I didn't feel he should have *anybody* on the paper.*

The Court (interrupting). You don't believe in having spies?

Rauh. No, sir.

Q. Unless they are your own?

A. Unless you are trying to uncover illegal activity which I was trying to do.

Q. You didn't think McCarthy was trying to uncover illegal activity?

A. No, I didn't.

Q. You thought you were the only one trying to do that?

A. I thought the *Washington Post* and I were the only ones trying to do that.

—leaving the fate of the country in a very few hands, the jurors must have thought.

—Had Rauh done anything he was ashamed of? He regretted, of course, having been taken in; nothing else. —What about the ethical problem of dealing with such a man as Hughes? Well, neither he nor Fritchey nor anyone else had known he was a confidence man.—But surely they knew from what Hughes himself said, that he was a shady character?—Had not both Rauh and Fritchey received from Hughes a hair-raising program of suggested action against Senator McCarthy in the teeth of which they formed their association?

Q. [Attorney for the Defense]. Do you recall whether Hughes at any time expressed any opinions which caused you seriously to doubt his ethics or morality?

Fritchey. No, not one single thing, no.

Excerpts from a memorandum to Clayton Fritchey by Hughes, dated December, 1953, and subsequently incorporated in the report prepared for Joe Rauh:

---

* Mr. Rauh has other views when it comes to the question whether loyalty risks should be allowed to hold down government jobs in nonsensitive positions.

Phone taps can be utilized [against McCarthy] . . . Don't discount the tremendous values in just bargaining power of recorded phone discussions . . . A program of this type, although not nice, can result in harm to no one except [McCarthy] . . . As mentioned earlier, being nice, too ethical, or squeamish, will accomplish less than nothing, where McCarthy is concerned. McCarthy has stated many times, "Ethics went out the window with buttoned shoes." So therefore I don't see the necessity for us (sic) to send a boy to do a man's work. If both federal and civil law enforcement agencies use the same unethical procedures to bring to justice criminals, are we not justified in using similar methods to expose [McCarthy] . . . ? It is most easy to prove and document [McCarthy's guilt] . . . by relaxing somewhat on ethics. This perhaps is probably what I'm best suited for. . .

Joe Rauh and Clayton Fritchey evidently agreed; and the great partnership was founded.

2.

In the course of the months to come, things got better and better. Getting reports from Paul Hughes was, for Joe Rauh—and for his friends Fritchey and Friendly—like taking dope. The dose had to be increased every time; and, always obliging, Paul Hughes always increased it. By the time the summer was well along, and their addiction complete, Hughes was driven to rather desperate measures to keep up the flow of information on the rascality of McCarthy. He had already tried, successfully, a melodramatic tale about how he had to move his wife and child to another state for fear that McCarthy, when he discovered he had been double-crossed, would send around some of his thugs to wipe out Hughes' family. And then, a few weeks later, he had tried to get money from Al Friendly of the *Washington Post* (who was acting as substitute paymaster while Rauh was in Europe)—to turn over, said Hughes, to an investigator on McCarthy's staff to be used by that investigator to buy off a girl he had gotten into trouble. But what did all this have to do with the *Washington Post,* he was asked. Obvious, said Hughes: by getting the investigator out of a jam, he could further ingratiate himself and get still *more* intimate secrets about the doings of McCarthy and the committee!

By midsummer, dizzied perhaps by an equatorial sun, Paul Hughes took a step which, notwithstanding a six-month run of steady successes, he must have deemed a little chancy. It must have been with a quiver of trepidation that he told his thirsting little group that Senator McCarthy and his staff had amassed an arsenal of pistols, lugers, and submachine guns in the basement of the Senate Office Building. Why? Well, *presumably* to protect themselves when they went out after evidence. But perhaps, Hughes must have hinted enticingly, for other reasons . . . (He knew from experience that his job was confined to the mere planting of seeds which a legion of neuroses could be counted on to water.)

Things became almost unbearably tense. A little later, Hughes told Friendly (Rauh was still out of town) that McCarthy was on the verge of sending someone to New York to pay cash for secret information snitched from the State Department by an employee. Here at last was an illegal act! Friendly got hold of his boss, Philip Graham, publisher of the *Washington Post,* and the two went hand-in-hand to the office of the Attorney General, Herbert Brownell, to tell him breathlessly that they had got hold of something hot. They couldn't tell him, they said, just what it was, but any day now it would happen; and he must hold himself ready, day and night, to put an FBI man at their disposal so that they could catch the lawbreaker *in flagrante.* They insisted on, and got, Brownell's unlisted home telephone number, so that they could reach him at whatever hour Hughes might call in.

Having secured Brownell's promise of help, the publisher and the editor of the *Washington Post* went back to the barricades to wait, anxiously, final word from

Hughes that the great illegal act for which they had all been praying and paying was about to take place.

Nothing happened.

After he had squeezed all the juice out of that one, advancing one reason after another why the rendezvous, week after week, did not come off (Hughes' excuse: Brownell must have told J. Edgar Hoover, Hoover must have guessed it involved McCarthy, Hoover must have tipped off McCarthy; whereupon McCarthy called off the operation), inventive little Paul Hughes simply went on to something else.

It went on, and on, and on. In October, the *Washington Post,* bracing itself for the climax, prepared twelve articles on Senator McCarthy, based on the information Paul Hughes had given it. And then, almost as an afterthought, a reporter, Murray Marder, was assigned to verify some of the information on the basis of which the *Post* was about to break into print. Marder went off to three or four employees of the Bell Telecommunications Laboratories (which manufacture secret equipment for the Signal Corps), whose "affidavits" testifying to the way in which McCarthy had browbeat them Hughes had furnished: and lo and behold, the workers didn't even exist! The affidavits the *Washington Post* was about to splash over the front pages were fictitious! It was in a state of near panic, one must suppose, that the researcher tore off to Cornell University, next stop on the verification tour, to interview a professor who, Paul Hughes had reported, had been blackmailed by McCarthy. If the professor refused to point an accusing finger at a few Communists on the Cornell faculty (never mind if they *were* Communist), McCarthy had allegedly threatened him, the Committee would publicly reveal that, in his misspent youth, the professor had sired an illegitimate son. Unlike the workers at the Bell Telecommunications Laboratories, the professor *did* exist; but he was very much startled by the story of his victimization. The poor old man had *never* been in touch with McCarthy or any member of McCarthy's committee, at any time; and on top of that, far from having misspent his youth, he had, the professor insisted stoutly, led a life of conspicuous rectitude.

The disappointment of the *Washington Post* must have been terrible. The series was killed. The bill was totted up: Hughes had collected over eight thousand dollars from Joseph Rauh, and over twenty-five hundred dollars from Clayton Fritchey; to say nothing of the consumption of hundreds and hundreds of valuable hours of some of the highest paid lawyers and publicists in Washington. Indignation flared.

But never out of control. The *Post* did *not* vent its indignation by publishing an exclusive story on the strange life and activities of an anti-McCarthy careerist. Joseph L. Rauh, Jr., his perfervid concern over law-breaking notwithstanding, did *not* report to the Justice Department the illegalities of a man who went about town getting money under false pretenses from credulous liberals, flashing forged credentials as an alleged member of a Senate Committee. Clayton Fritchey did *not* complain to the police that Hughes had subsequently tried to blackmail him. General Cornelius Mara did *not* complain that Hughes had given him a bum check. No, these forgiving men were prepared just to let Hughes recede from memory.

But the irrepressible Mr. Hughes would not cooperate. He looked around for fresh bait—and decided to con the FBI, much as Raffles decided, finally, to have a go at the Crown jewels. From that point on, his career moved to a rapid end. On the basis of what he told the FBI, he was subpoenaed by a grand jury, and in due course the government decided to prosecute him for lying before that jury. The government was confident it would win a conviction. It saw no reason to doubt that a person who *admitted* to being a *professional* liar could be proved to have lied, in these specific instances, to a grand jury. But the government prosecutors overlooked one thing: in order to prove that Hughes was a liar, it had to prove that Rauh, Friendly, and Fritchey were *not* liars. That proved an insurmountable obstacle. With the result that, today, Hughes is a free man.*

3.

I do not pretend that the recounting of the essential facts of the Hughes episode does not afford a wry amusement. For Rauh and company had for years moralized about the venality of the secret informer—even when used under sanction of custom, law, and relevant administrative rulings, subject, in the end, to all judicial safeguards. Now it developed that even while they were loudly condemning the use of "political spies" and "secret informers," they were themselves making deliberate, extended, and blanket use of a man whom they believed to be a political spy and secret informer—one who, moreover, had told them explicitly and in writing that he was not merely being personally disloyal to his employer, but was prepared to use illegal methods to get his alleged information.

But I do not recount the Hughes story merely to chronicle a great hypocrisy. There is much to be learned from the Hughes case and its aftermath—particularly if one bears in mind that Joseph L. Rauh, Jr. (I name him as a matter of convenience; one must not forget the

---

* The indictment of Paul Hughes was on six counts of alleged perjury committed in testimony before a Federal Grand Jury in 1955. The first four counts cited statements made by Hughes to the effect that Joseph L. Rauh, Jr., *et al.*, had discussed Harvey Matusow during 1954. The last two counts concerned Hughes' statement to the Grand Jury that Rauh was aware that Hughes' representation of himself as a McCarthy secret investigator was false, and that Hughes' reports on McCarthy's doings were doctored. On February 3, 1956, the jury acquitted Hughes on the first two counts of the indictment and was "hung" (unable to reach a unanimous verdict) on the remaining four counts. A juror subsequently reported that the division on count 3 was 6–6, and 11–1 in favor of acquittal on the other three. In November of 1958, the government recommended that Hughes not be retried, and gave its reason: "During the trial the credibility of the major government witnesses was severely attacked by its defense . . . There is no reason to believe that a second jury would be any less receptive to the contentions made by the defense." An official opinion on the credibility, before a jury of their peers, of Joseph L. Rauh, Jr., Alfred Friendly, and Clayton Fritchey.

company of persons involved in the Hughes operation) is a rewarding object of attention by anyone seeking to understand the operations of the liberal mind. Let us always remember that not *one* liberal publicist—not one, I should say, that I know of—expressed disapproval of Rauh by condemning his affiliation with Paul Hughes. Not the editorial writers of the *New York Times,* the *New York Post,* or the *New York Herald Tribune* (the *Washington Post* and *New York Post* were of course compelled to publish brief, self-serving editorials and, dutifully, did so); not the Alsops, or Marquis Childs, or Roscoe Drummond, or Doris Fleeson, or Drew Pearson, or Thomas Stokes, or Richard Rovere.* This must mean either that they saw nothing in that behavior to criticize, or that fraternal loyalty to a fellow ideologue prevailed over the sense of duty. The former hypothesis is especially interesting. It would seem clear that Rauh's enthusiastic use, in pursuit of anti-Communists, of methods whose use in pursuit of pro-Communists he persistently denounces, is a measure of his evaluation of the relative threat (and relative objectionability?) of the two forces. And indeed, spokesmen for liberalism have often insisted that anti-Communism is more dangerous to America than Communism. But the reason usually advanced for making such a claim is that anti-Communists tend to use despicable, totalitarian methods. Like secret informers. If the same spokesmen are prepared to sanction the use of such methods to persecute politically offensive persons, what grounds have they left on which to oppose the anti-Communists whose *methods,* they say (as distinguished from their aims) render them objectionable?

A week after Paul Hughes was freed I pondered the question, more relevant now than ever: What can one

---

* When *National Review,* shortly after the conclusion of the trial, chided liberal publicists for not commenting on the case, Rovere wrote me: "I agree with you that the Hughes case is full of import . . . I know that I shall deal with the Hughes case in (my forthcoming book)." The forthcoming book turned out to be *Senator Joe McCarthy* (Harcourt Brace, 1959). It contains not a single mention of Paul Hughes.

75

do to kindle in the liberal bosom a spirit of antagonism toward the Communists equal in intensity to that which moved the liberals to fight against Senator McCarthy? The horror of the philosophical postulates of Communism has not sufficed, nor the horror of Communism's historical record. What then? I wrote: "A few years ago a sardonic observer indulged in a little wishful thinking. 'If only,' he said, 'Mao Tse-tung, back in 1946 or 1947, had criticized Margaret Truman's singing! China might have been saved!' We cannot, it seems, count on the hideousness of Communism to instill in us the will to fight back. Something else will have to furnish the impulse. Perhaps some day, in his cups, Nikita Khrushchev, moved to repay a long outstanding diplomatic courtesy, will sputter out, 'You know, I like old Joe—McCarthy, that is.' Then will the liberals mount their chargers, and join the fray, prepared to shed their blood to devastate the newly discovered enemy."

THE LIBERAL—And the Obliging Order

OUR AGE OF MODULATION

THERE ARE SEVERAL reasons why, in recent years, the discussion process in America appears to have broken down. The principal reason is the emphatic indisposition by those whose views prevail in critical quarters to accept any challenge to their intellectual hegemony, to recognize dissent from their conformity as serious. But another factor that militates against purposive discourse is the developing taboo first on strong opinions, second on their expression in relentless language. During the Eisenhower years, ours became a land of lotus-eaters, the gates to which are guarded by the dragons I have described. The tendency, these days, is to yield to the passion for modulation. Even in literature, one does not often find oneself concerned with kings and knaves, fair maidens and heroes, treachery and honor, right and wrong; one speaks in greys, and muted hues, of social problems, and life adjustment, and co-existence and intercredal amity. Increasingly, we are called upon to modulate our voices. Increasingly, the convention of tact brings us to modulate not only our voices, but also our dogmas.

Social life is not possible in the absence of certain restraints; that is obvious. There are the clearly indicated restraints which, for example, impel us to respect our neighbor's life and property. There are the more indirect, the more subtle restraints, that aim, ambitiously, at looking after not only our neighbor's life and property, but his sensibilities as well. It is this concern for sensibilities that gave birth to the euphemism; for it set into motion the search for the softer word, the blunted explanation, the circumlocution aimed at mitigating the harshness of a conclusion, or an evaluation. Thus we address our bitterest enemies "Dear Sir," and speak of "passing away" when we mean dying; of "detention" when we mean imprisonment; of "underdeveloped" when we mean primitive; of "retarded" when we mean half-witted; of "idealistic" when we mean confused; of "unaware" when we should mean ignorant.

Many of these modulations go hand in hand with a civilized respect for the feelings of others. But I suspect diplomacy has got out of hand. The compulsion to soften can be seen elbowing out the desire to make oneself clear. Professor Ralph Gabriel of Yale has written that advertising in America grew from a "chatty little industry in the twenties to a cosmic urge in the thirties." The same holds true of the public relations industry. The modulated approach threatens to overwhelm reality and truth. The human impulse to be tactful evolutionizes into a tendency to refuse to acknowledge facts; and, ultimately, into the taking of liberties with metaphysical properties. An indiscriminate gentility can induce relativism, and relativism can be blind. Compulsive gentility has far-reaching moral consequences.

The Japanese, we all know, are renowned for their good manners. It is a part of the Japanese tradition to exhibit great modesty, to disparage one's accomplishments, to deprecate, even, one's most sacred opinions. To this end they use, in their day-to-day speech, many self-effacing conventions which, transliterated into English, are startling to say the least. A Japanese is said to have introduced himself to an American beside whom he was seated at an international inter-religious conference by saying, "My miserable superstition is Buddhism. What is yours?" In that wonderful remark is the zany convergence of tact and capitulation. From there, at this colloquy, it could have gone either way.

What is it that led from the civility that tradition

dictates be shown to one's neighbor, regardless of our differences with him, to a camaraderie, in the name of Tolerance, with, say, a Communist? What was that it parlayed the conviction that it is desirable for men of diverse political faiths to live on the same planet together, into the conviviality that has marked recent meetings between representatives of East and West? When did tact and sympathy for backward students become institutionalized in a school system that refuses in effect to recognize the existence of advanced students? What exactly is the source of that hypertoleration that makes acceptable such observations as Mrs. Roosevelt's in a memorable column? ("I was shocked to hear that not long ago, in one of our schools, some older boys beat up their teacher. When this happens, you can be sure that the blame does not lie with the young people . . .")

It is hard to say. But as when seeking to understand any phenomenon, one looks to the academies for leads. There is no handy explanation for the national compulsion to suffuse all unpleasant facts with undifferentiated and well-meaning irrelevancies; but there are factors bearing on the phenomenon that are worth looking into.

Those factors are highly elusive, and for an understanding of them one leans not so much on analysts and statisticians, as on men of poetic intuition. A successful novelist can do more to identify a national social tendency, or syndrome, than a dozen technicians. The late Professor Randall Jarrell wrote a novel of wit and trenchancy, to which I have already referred, which is far too little known or appreciated; a novel that has a look at some of the mannerisms and malignancies of triumphant liberalism.*

1.

Randall Jarrell writes of life and manners at "Benton College." Benton College is a swish girls' college, very, very serious about things, very dedicated, devotedly

* *Pictures From an Institution,* New York, Alfred A. Knopf, 1954.

Enlightened, and consumingly Tolerant. At Benton there were girls from every economic and social group. A great many rich girls, to be sure, but there were many more who were just comfortably well-to-do; and there were poor girls, too, on scholarships . . .

And there were what I [the narrator] used to call to myself token students: black students, brown students, yellow students, students who were believers of the major creeds of Earth—one or two of each. If there is in Tierra del Fuego a family of fire-worshippers with a daughter of marriageable age, and a couple of thousand dollars a year to spare, they can educate her at Benton.

What is the first objective at this archetype of higher liberal learning in mid-century America? Why, it is to reach in deep and disturb the waters of conviction. A student must be saved from the superstitions she brings with her to Benton; saved from the petty little delusions she gets from her parents, from her faith, or from tradition in general. At Benton College the education of the girls is "what the girls themselves would have called a traumatic experience." The school psychologists talked of education "not simply as therapy but as shock therapy: 'The first thing I do with a freshman,' one of them said to Dr. Rosenbaum [the music professor], 'is to shake her out of her ignorant complacency.' Dr. Rosenbaum knew one of [the freshmen in question] . . . , a cheerful scatterbrained girl who was neither cheerful nor scatterbrained about her psychology teacher; this girl said viciously, 'All she does is *pry*. She thinks I'm a bourgeois prejudice and she wants me to get rid of myself.' "

And having brought on this traumatic experience, the educators of Benton simply let the student go. They do not deliver her into the arms of Marx, or into any organized philosophical system; they simply turn her loose. When she graduates, she knows that our civilization is gross, and insensitive, and inadequate, but she doesn't know exactly where to turn . . .

If Benton had had an administration building with pillars, it could have carved over the pillars: "Ye shall know the truth, and the truth shall make you feel guilty." Just as ordinary animal awareness has been replaced in many by consciousness, so consciousness had been replaced, in most of the teachers of Benton, by social consciousness. They were successful in teaching most of their students to say in contrition about anything whatsoever: *It was I, Lord, it was I;* but they were not so successful in teaching them to consider this consciousness of guilt a *summum bonum,* one's final claim upon existence. Many a Benton girl went back to her nice home, married her rich husband—and carried a fox in her bosom for the rest of her life—and short of becoming a social worker, founding a Neo-Socialist party, and then killing herself and leaving her insurance to the United Nations, I do not know how she could have got rid of it.

What kind of people teach at Benton, and administer Benton education? Let us look at four of them. Consider Mr. Daudier, the man of letters, with his precious devotion to other civilizations. Mr. Jarrell describes Mr. Daudier as . . .

a prominent literary critic: he had a column of criticism every week except the last two weeks in August, in the best-known literary weekly . . . During the school year he would lecture to colleges and when the school year was over, he would make commencement addresses to them or get honorary degrees from them; he was the chief reader of a publishing house, he was one of the vice-presidents of the American branch of the *Académie Française;* you saw one-act plays by him, if you fell among anthologies of one-act plays; he even wrote informal essays . . . He didn't know anything about, or care anything for, science, unless it was several hundred years old—or several thousand, for choice; he loved it then. He would say, 'What do we know that Aristotle didn't know?' But he wouldn't let you tell him; it was a rhetorical question. He had diabetes and used to get an injection of insulin every day, but I

81

don't believe he ever got one without wishing it was Galen giving it to him. There were two things he was crazy about, the thirteenth century and Greek; if the thirteenth century had spoken Greek I believe it would have killed him not to have been alive in it.

What kind of man presides over Benton College? Well, President Robbins embodies every one of the qualities of the Modulated Age. He is Mr. Public Relations himself. Consider his Commencement Address . . .

President Robbins made a speech that——that——as Gertrude [the protagonist] said, you had to hear it not to believe it. When he finished, he finished by thanking the students, parents, and faculty of Benton for the experience of working with, of learning from, and of growing to . . . love . . . such generous and intelligent, such tolerant and understanding, such— and here he paused quite a long time—such . . . good . . . people. As he said . . . *good* . . . there was in his voice so radiant a freshness, so yearning a transfiguration of all created things that the audience rose from their seats and sang out like Sieglinde: *Thou art the Spring!* No, they didn't actually, insensate things, but they wanted to: you could look at them and see that they were Changed.

Or consider President Robbins out on the road, collecting money:

His appeals for funds were nowhere more successful than in Hollywood. Several Benton alumnae were stars, socially-conscious script-writers, wives or daughters of producers. President Robbins appealed to them sitting in somewhat Hawaiian swimming-shorts at the grassy verge of swimming-pools; as he looked thoughtfully into the thoughtless water he seemed to the alumnae some boyish star who, playing Tom Sawyer, fancies for the moment that he is Narcissus. Not to have given him what he asked, they felt, would have been to mine the bridge that bears the train that carries the supply of this year's Norman Rockwell Boy Scout Calendars.

Tolerance, of course, is everybody's major at Benton College. Not everyone can hope to be as tolerant as Flo, the wife of the professor of architecture; but everyone should aspire to be, for Flo is deeply committed to what she calls Real Life . . .

> Almost everything that happened to Flo and her family and her friends was, after all, only private; and to her *real life* was public, what you voted at or gave for, or read about in the *Nation*. Life seemed to Flo so petty, compared to real life. The trouble with women, people say, is that they take everything personally; Flo took nothing personally. If she had been told that Benton College, and [her husband] Jerrold, and [her son] John, and [her daughter] Fern, *and* their furniture had been burned to ashes by the head of the American Federation of Labor, who had then sown salt over the ashes, she would have sobbed and said, at last—she could do no other—"I think that we ought to hear *his* side of the case before we make up our minds."

So, finally, what kind of girls graduate from Benton? Well, to describe them is beyond the powers even of Mr. Jarrell. He makes a valiant attempt, but gives up . . .

> Most of the people of Benton would have swallowed a porcupine, if you had dyed its quills and called it Modern Art . . . they were *so* liberal and selfless, politically, that—but what words of men, or tongue of man or angel, can one find adequate to this great theme?

2.

Now no one can deny that Randall Jarrell was having himself a whale of a time—or be anything less than grateful that he should have let us in on the merriment. But he was also saying, forgive the expression (Flo would have understood it), Serious Things. He was describing a morally and intellectually deracinated environment in which students are encouraged to cut their ties to the world of standards and norms, to march forward as soldiers of a totemic tolerance—like Flo; permanently committed to the insufficiency of our own society—like the girl who in order to find Peace must name the United Nations her beneficiary; factitiously obsessed with another civilization (any other civilization) and another age (any other age)—like Mr. Daudier; smooth and urbane—and empty, like President Robbins.

Well, American college graduates don't come out exactly that way, of course, as everybody knows. But it is often through parody that the artist succeeds in getting a near-photographic likeness. And out of this fantasy, one can distill the essence of what goes into shaping the men and women who *are* typical of our age, the men and women whose views tend to prevail in America; the liberals.

Dwight Eisenhower, symbol of the modulated age, did not go to Benton, and in fact he would be much despised there, though mostly for the wrong reasons. Nonetheless, he was a serviceable symbol of the modulated age, the age which, by their agnosticism, the Bentons of the land have assiduously promoted. The conscious philosophical relativism of the academy, filtering down past the scholars and the intelligentsia to the masses, becomes less a *Weltanschauung,* more an attitude of mind. It is the prevalence of this attitude of mind that made it possible for Modern Republicanism to pause, triumphant, on its way to Limbo; that attitude made it possible for Dwight Eisenhower to attain a level of personal popularity no president had known since James Madison. The liberal ideology is programmatic in a sense in which the Republicanism of Mr. Eisenhower definitely is not. But the two, in time and place, are highly compatible; for encompassed by the blandness of Modern Republicanism, the stimulation of intellectual and political resistance to the continuing liberal offensive is all but impossible—as recent elections have shown.

It was the dominating ambition of Eisenhower's Modern Republicanism to govern in such fashion as to more or less please more or less everybody. Such governments must shrink from principle: because principles have edges, principles cut; and blood is drawn, and people get hurt. And who would hurt anyone in an age of modulation?

The struggle in those days, if that is the word for it, was toward blandness; toward a national euphoria. Leadership consists of giving the people everything they want—and, if they are caught not wanting enough, reminding them of all the things they should be wanting (except the right things). Dwight Eisenhower was the proper instrument of such an age. Everything is, for him, personal; there is little of objective, super-personal importance. In the three speeches in his presidential career in which he spoke his mind spontaneously, exuberantly—on the dramatic occasions when he announced, freshly arisen from his sickbed, his decision to run again; when he spoke to the voters on election eve, in 1956; and again the next evening when he exulted over his election—he spoke only of himself. In the half hour during which he announced to the nation that he would run again despite his recent illness, there was no time to refer to a nation and a world in crisis. For in his eyes there is no really serious crisis. And if there is one, something called the Eisenhower Program would wish it away. Let us not have dire and embarrassing talk, Eisenhower and everyone else seemed to be saying, about a need for heroic exertions, about the stabbing cries that issue forth out of the darkness to which one half of the world is perpetually committed; for these are times of cheer, of plenty, of warmheartedness, of blurred images and diffuse sentimentality: the era of the Eisenhower Program.

Mr. Eisenhower always had difficulty in describing the nature of the Eisenhower program, and it is a difficulty traceable to something more subtle than the devil-syntax that has always plagued him. The most expensive professional verbalizers in his entourage had much the same trouble. So that when the Eisenhower program, in conception and practice, was described, however enthusiastically, however ingeniously, or neatly, it nevertheless refused to reduce to an orderly system of political or philosophical beliefs, or even to a consistent set of axioms or definitions concerning the nature of the problem at hand, or how to deal with it.

What was the Eisenhower Program?

Was it a Program which as a matter of policy sought out the middle of the road? Mr. Eisenhower himself has so intimated—adding ruefully, that "it takes great courage to follow the middle" against constant attack from both the left and the right. But Eisenhower's sharpest defenders would make no such concession. For it is indispensable to the program that it irradiate a moral purpose; and middle-of-the-road qua middle-of-the-road is morally insecure, as the first Republican President warned at Cooper Union.*

The objectives of the Eisenhower Program? They were hard to name. What are the objectives of the housewife next door? To get on with her workday chores, to continue to exercise a certain influence and control over the household, to like, and be liked, to contribute to the general tranquility—and, always, to live yet another day. Most of what goes on in the world has no discernible "objective."

The Eisenhower Program was no exception. Essentially it was an attitude, which went by the name of program, undirected by principle, unchained to any coherent idea as to the nature of man and society, uncommitted to any sustained estimate of the nature or potential of the enemy. Yet because of the sincerity of its leader and the ingenuity and devotion of its publicists, it was a Program which, whatever it was up to at any given moment, took on the air of moral justification and intellectual tightness. The Program suffered from the ultimate lifelessness of any program unanimated by definition or principle, but it possessed, too, a marvelous

---

* "Let us be diverted," said Lincoln, "by none of those sophistical contrivances wherewith we are so industriously plied and belabored —contrivances such as groping for some middle ground between the right and the wrong."

flexibility. It could respond quickly, and decisively, to the slightest political impulse, and it could even reconcile opposites. Under the Eisenhower Program one could, simultaneously, declare for a free market economy and veto such as the gas bill which aimed at a free market on gas; stand by a policy of liberation and go to Geneva; lucubrate over constitutional rights and freedoms and forever abandon captured American soldiers; and over the whole package—and this was Mr. Eisenhower's historical skill—there was suffused a general benignity of a kind that bewitched the multitude of the voters. Even though there were included in that multitude legions of men and women who, in their own moral and intellectual lives, live according to the Word, and see things as they are.

3.

Here, indeed, is a danger distinctive to our time, one that transcends the danger of profound strategic mis-reckonings as to the power or intentions of the enemy, and transcends, too, the danger of a casual institutional-ization of the statist measures and paraphernalia which sometimes go by the name of "creeping socialism." In seeking out the bland, the modulated approach, in blur-ring distinctions, and in acclimatizing men to life with-out definition, we erode the Western position; and that, take or leave a few bombs and airplanes, is all we have got. The nihilist tidal wave continues to build up power, and it is on the move. Effective resistance to it will call for supreme individual and collective exertion. But in behalf of what will this exertion be made? The Eisen-hower program? The Great Society? A nation, to be loved, must be lovely, Burke said; and a position, to be effectively defended against the appeal of a utopian-materialist order, against the connivings and sacrifices of millions of active partisans who aim at the hearts and minds of every individual on earth—a position that can stand up under all that must be clear, and bright, and intact; it cannot, after prolonged abuse by aimless mushheadedness, generate the will to stand, resolute, against forces that history itself seems to be championing. Who will nail the theses on Communism's church door? Chester Bowles?

There is something to be said for breaking away from modulation's trance; for straight thought, and straight talk, even of the kind which, on account of its directness, is capable of lifting people right out of their chairs; the kind of talk that will risk for the talker the reputation of being impolitic and ungenteel. At a crowded reception at the Kremlin in the early 1930's, Lady Astor turned to Stalin and asked, "When are you going to stop killing people?" Bishop Sheen once called up Heywood Broun, whom he had never met but whose nihilistic columns he read every day, and told him he wanted to see him. "What about?" asked Broun gruffly. "About your soul," said Bishop Sheen.

Now everybody knows you shouldn't talk about gibbets to executioners, especially not when they happen also to be heads of State. And who, having read the literature of decorum, will, in conversation with sinners, bring up the subject of hell? Still, etiquette is the first value only of the society that has no values, the effete society. An occasional disregard for the niceties may bring us face to face with certain facts from which, in his obsessive search for equanimity, man labors to shield himself. Such facts as that Stalin was a murderer, and Broun a cynic; such as that some boys are thugs, and that though there never was any practicable way of preventing Mrs. Roosevelt from extending her compassion to them when they were moved to beat up their teacher, we might at least have arranged to forward her mash notes to them to some reformatory. Such facts as that one half of the inhabitants of the world are in chains, living on a perpetual diet of misery, and that to encourage social and cultural traffic with their tormentors calls for a kind of callousness no society can practice, and still think of itself as civilized.

Such facts as the Original Sin cannot be made to disappear, even by action of the General Assembly of the

United Nations; that human beings are not equal, cannot be made equal, and must not be deemed equal other than before the law; such facts as that excellence can be distinguished from mediocrity, and that precocity is not an affront on democratic society. The recognition of these facts, and scores of others, is the indispensable weapon of self-defense against the ideologists. Our mania for a comatose togetherness keeps these facts remote from view.

Let those who understand this to be a call to Intolerance bear in mind the dictum of Etienne Gilson: tolerance is a meaningless concept except as practiced by a fervent believer. How can the modern relativist exercise tolerance if he doesn't believe in anything to begin with? It is not hard to exhibit toleration toward a point of view if you have no point of view of your own with which that point of view conflicts. It is the man who believes, and only he, who is capable of exhibiting the virtue of tolerance.

Even then, the balance is often off. We all know men who believe firmly in a set of principles, but for whom it appears to be more important to display an exemplary tolerance toward those who disagree, than to affirm their own beliefs. Surely one should stand by one's views, evenly and quietly, even if in doing so it becomes necessary to rend the stillness of sweet modulation.

I recall with pleasure a dialogue several years ago between the journalist Ralph de Toledano and his publishers. They had sent Toledano the proof sheets on his latest novel. In going over them he noticed that wherever the word Heaven or the word Hell appeared, they had not been capitalized, as the manuscript had prescribed, but appeared instead in small letters. Toledano painstakingly corrected each of them, elevating them once again to upper case; and sent back the proofs. He received a telephone call. "Ralph," said the publisher, "we have a set of style rules over here we must observe. Why do you insist on capitalizing Heaven and Hell?" "Because," replied Toledano evenly, "they're places. You know, like Scarsdale."

THE LIBERAL—And the Silent Generation

THE DECLINE OF PARTISANSHIP

IN THE WINTER OF 1958, the Stanford University *Daily,* having done some routine editorializing on student apathy, one by one ticking off, and rejecting, the standard explanations for that apathy, arrived at a painful conclusion: "The only logical reason we can think of as the cause of student dullness is that we *are* dull."

The charge should be specified. Most students, I think, *have* become dull in their political aspect. That is to say, they are uninterested in the political world, and therefore uninteresting when they creak their minds to it. And too often those students who are politically minded behave as though they had taken perpetual vows of banality. This may be the fault of our political system, where success seems more and more to require the ruthless suppression of intellectual or rhetorical discrimination.

I doubt that students are, in fact, any less energetic now than they were in other years. The ergs they devote to daily existence are probably not fewer than at other times; perhaps they are greater, since standards of nutrition have risen. The most highly neglected dimension of politics, these days, is politics as art, as entertainment, as melodrama. Schedule a really hot debate, and students will come out of the woodwork to hear it. Let them anticipate either a) high forensic or dialectical skill (e.g., the polished Professor Fred Rodell of Yale vs. the formidable James Jackson Kilpatrick on the subject of the Supreme Court); or b) a crushing personal defeat for one or the other contestant (e.g., McGeorge Bundy vs. an outclassed Allan Zoll on "Academic Freedom"); or c) a piquant personal situation (Owen Lattimore vs. Freda Utley, on "Was the I. P. R. or wasn't it communist dominated")—sometimes the fires that are kindled at such meetings stay lit. But this is really what political life on the campus seems to have reduced to: a few spectaculars. One wonders why? Is it because of the total ascendancy of a particular set of ideas? Or is it because of the nature of the ideas that *have* triumphed?

It persists in sounding just a little unreal, but the record is there: in the twenties and thirties (as we are often reminded) Ivy League debate teams exercised themselves before packed audiences in theaters in downtown Boston. Two law students at Yale, maddened by the foreign policy of Franklin Roosevelt, founded the America First Committee, which in two years enrolled fifteen million members. All of Columbia University turned out at a rally protesting the firing of Reed Harris as editor of the Columbia *Spectator*.

I witnessed what evidently was the last gasp of campuswide political consciousness during my freshman year at Yale, in 1946. The campus teemed with ideologues-on-the-march, and their leaders occupied the center of the stage, *ex officio*. I remember the undergraduate president of the American Veterans Committee announcing *at a press conference* (imagine the head of the A. V. C. having the effrontery to call a press conference nowadays!) that it was by no means to be taken for granted that the A. V. C. would countenance the University's announced rise in the tuition rate—he and his executive committee would reflect on the matter, and pass judgment upon it in due course. And all this nonsense would be duly chronicled in apocalyptic headlines in the undergraduate paper!

But it did not last; it ended, indeed, even before the

year was out, and though there were some glorious political rows at Yale in the next few years, one had the feeling that they were sustained by an old battery, capable, still, of photoflash charges of energy, but left gasping for breath by the exorbitant demands on its waning powers.

1.

And then came the more or less official epitaph: ours was the Silent Generation; the generation of conformist, security-conscious, drab, unexciting young people.

It seems to me the postwar generation, the first, I gather, brought up under a consolidated liberalism, had a lot to be silent about. An explicit objection was made in 1958 to the designation by the Princeton seniors who recited their world-views in a volume called, by its editor, *The Unsilent Generation*. Everybody knows that one cannot loosen the tongue of an entire generation by merely producing a book, however talkative, by individual members of that generation; and anyway, those who read the externalizations of the dozen students who wrote the book may be prepared, given the circumstances, to settle for Silence. Rather silence, I would vote, than this dismaying—though fascinating—book.

Murray Kempton called *The Unsilent Generation* "the *Atlas Shrugged* of the liberals"; by which he meant that the component parts of liberalism are, in the words and thoughts of the typical contributor to this volume, driven to gruesome extreme. Mr. Francis Horn, reviewing the book for the *New York Times,* recalled an undergraduate Dartmouth song which begins "Don't send my son to Princeton/The dying mother said"—and predicted the ditty would climb to the Hit Parade; by which he meant that the book so strikingly demonstrates the bleakness of the Princeton experience as to make Princeton education a national concern. The irrepressible Father Halton, who was Chaplain to Catholic students at Princeton, quipped that President Goheen was not likely, on the evidence of this book, to allow any of his

92

daughters to go out with members of the unsilent generation; a reference to the casual sexual attitudes of some of the contributors to the book. The publisher found embodied in the slender volume the "temper, the moral attitudes, the credos, and the aspirations of young people today"; by which he meant one should buy the book.

I agree that one should. It is wrong to suggest (as was widely done) that to examine the book, and the inner thoughts of twelve Princeton seniors, is like reading Krafft-Ebing. One can justifiably resist most generalizations about the younger generation that are here and there suggested by the book. Those who see in the book evidence of intellectual mediocrity would have a difficult time explaining the eleventh contributor, who is a young man of luminous intelligence, of highly developed powers of understanding and synthesis. Conformist? Number 7 is close to being an anarchist (he even disapproves of government paternalism!)—though there are worrisome signs that he will end up more crank than individualist. Skeptical? Number 5 has not lost his religion, is a fervent Christian; Number 9 also believes in some sort of God. Egalitarian? Number 2 was brought up to think of himself as "a gentleman and a gentleman's son" and in four thousand of the iciest words I have ever read, affirms his title, by the rules of natural selection, to membership in the elite—(only he calls it, as one would expect from an idiomatic Princeton senior, "the liberal elite.") Inarticulate? Number 6 writes with skill. Frivolous? Number 9 is deeply wise, serenely understanding.

Even so, the book yields a net impression which is a desolate one indeed, and closely related to the nature of liberalism.

Higher education today emphasizes the development of the critical faculties—though to what purpose is not clear; and that it is not clear is the central revelation of the contemporary critique of higher education. Although it is tacitly agreed that all graduates of Princeton shall be faithful servants of liberalism, it is not clear what liberalism is, because liberalism is not really anything substantive; and even if it were, any enrollment in such an order would, under academic freedom, have to remain inexplicit. Princeton (and the same is true of other colleges) would never be caught corporately urging a dedication of the intellectual faculties to the service of a particular world view. Such a thing being, in an age of relativism, unmodish, and in any case, proscribed by the rites of academic freedom.

But what strikes one most in this book is not so much the Bentonian sense of insufficiency as the related feeling of personal powerlessness, projected at every level. If God exists, one student wrote, what has that to do with me? He cannot influence me, and I cannot influence Him: "I figure I can be indifferent to an indifferent God." What can I do about the march of history? another student asks rhetorically. He can do nothing, he means us to understand; no one can. The great events of the modern world are shaped by forces that individual human beings cannot influence. Great events are for great bureaucracies, and sociologists, to deal with. Political tidal waves are not deflected by the exertion of individual wills. The great Churchill himself was not able to cope with Communism. Man's destiny is wrought on a billion roof gardens; that is why personal statecraft is boring, and mechanized. And why the speculation in this book by twelve Princeton seniors is so appallingly egocentric, and why so much of it deals with grubby little matters that seldom intimate the capacity of the human spirit.

The impression *The Unsilent Generation* leaves, in a word, is one of egomania. And if one's interest in oneself is obsessive, that helps to account for an impatience with activities in which public policy is the focal concern. There is, of course, personal satisfaction to be derived from having a hand in the shaping of events. But a phenomenon of our age has been that fatalistic sense of personal remoteness from the mechanisms of public policy. Another phenomenon, the more important one, is the lack of conviction, and therefore the lack of partisanship, that has resulted from reigning philosophical notions about truth. Taken together, the two phenomena are enough to numb the political impulses of most people.

2.

It seems to me that there will not again be a robust political life in the undergraduate world until the student becomes convinced that *it matters* what he thinks about public problems. After the war the world appeared to be in flux, and from all over hands reached out, straining to leave individual marks on the clay—quick, before it hardened. Students went about the campus weighted down by a macrocosmic concern for the human race. As ever, most of the nostrum-peddlers pointed Left: we must nationalize the railroads, inaugurate world government, throw our bombs into the sea. But there were those, also, who spoke out against all that. The point is, there was wide political concern (some of it with a wonderfully zany edge*). It was generally believed that every individual exertion, every point scored, every pamphlet distributed, every polemic delivered, contributed to the crystallization of an historical impulse. So the halls were full, the oratory urgent and animated, the journalism spirited.

And then, very soon, reality closed in. It became clear that student sentiment could not persuade a Tito to stay the execution of a Mihailovich; more, that student protest would not persuade the State Department to persuade Tito to spare Mihailovich; worse, that student sentiment would not persuade local congressmen to persuade the State Department to persuade Tito . . . And, since we are a practical people, the question inevitably arose: if we are not going to have a visible

---

* One irrepressible senior, who did not care aught for ideology, but was bent on cashing in on those political impulses, announced that after graduation he would launch a firm, Foreign Relations, Inc., to take over, on a monthly fee basis, the foreign policy of sovereign states; the idea being to get at national objectives scientifically.

influence on events through our political agitations, are they worth the trouble? In other times the answer would have been an emphatic Yes—a stubborn, idealistic refusal to concede the pointlessness, the irrelevance, of individual effort, an idealism fortified by the conviction that even if the uselessness of an effort is absolutely establishable, the ethical imperative is there—and one must fight, if only to have fought.

But to take such a view one must feel deeply; and that, notoriously, the silent generation does not do.

3.

Why? I think the answer lies in the prevailing view of things in the average college. We don't feel deeply because there are no fixed, acknowledged norms by which, taking the measure of our deviation, we grasp and then insist upon the need for reform. What norms there are, are merely conventional. They are not rooted in the natural order. The big excitement at Yale in the fall of 1958, in connection with a student protest addressed to Khrushchev against the handling of Boris Pasternak, was over the question whether Americans were morally licensed to issue such an objection! If the Soviet Union persecutes its intellectuals (never mind that it is for writing the truth), the students assembled concluded, it is no different from a congressional committee's persecuting an intellectual (never mind that it is for writing error). Truth? Error? These are strange words, atavistic words. Granted the average student can be counted on to smell out the phoniness of the argument (so assiduously labored by the ideologues), that America is as guilty as the Soviet Union in the matter of bringing intellectuals to heel. Left to their own devices, they would yield to common sense, and acknowledge a qualitative difference between, say, Columbia's handling of Professor Gene Weltfish, and Russia's of Shostakovitch.

Still, they wonder, What is the theoretical base from which to talk back to the proposition that Persecution is Persecution, and that's all there is to it? They grope because prevailing preoccupations are with *method*, not *substance;* and so by a little dialectical artfulness, i.e., by a properly measured ascent up the ladder of generalization, one can group together generically the treatment of Pasternak and Lattimore under the classification: The Showing of Displeasure by an Agency of Government Toward an Intellectual. Completely irrelevant is the cause of the government's displeasure, or the legitimacy of the government whose displeasure is incurred. If evil and good are merely conventional words, the student is left only with the fact of harassment to weigh; not the cause of it.

How can one feel passionately about method? And what is it other than method that one is encouraged, in the relativist academic surroundings of liberalism, to feel passionately about? There was much more excitement over Senator McCarthy's methods (did he or did he not, in his interrogation of Civil Servant Jones, observe approved methods of interrogation?)—than over the putative revelations that ensued upon the interrogation (did Civil Servant Jones in fact whisk away that atomic secret?). There are many more allusions, in college campuses, to the fact that Antonio Salazar governs Portugal undemocratically—than to the fact that he has governed it well. (Can't you hear it?—"How *can* you govern well if you don't govern democratically?") The central concern of higher liberal education being for method, *qua* method, the excitement, when there is any, is over method: over Democracy—not "is democracy yielding desirable results"? Over Academic Freedom—not is "academic freedom advancing the truth"? Over Scientific Method—not "where is it applicable"? Over Education—not "what shall we teach"?

Democracy, as I shall emphasize in the succeeding chapter, has no eschatology; no vision, no fulfillment, no point of arrival. Neither does academic freedom. Both are merely instruments, the one supposed to induce a harmonious society, the second supposed to advance knowledge. Now let me say that I, for one, would not willingly die for "democracy," any more than I would willingly die for "academic freedom." I do understand the disposition to die for the kind of society democracy sometimes ushers in; and I do understand the willingness to die in behalf of some of the truths academic freedom may have been instrumental in apprehending. There is the difference. It is not lost on the undergraduate or on the adult public that there is no liberal vision. And so long as there is not, there is no call for the passionate commitments that stir the political blood.

It is not inconsistent that professional leaders of political liberalism should so exert themselves as, for example, a Joseph Rauh will do against a McCarthy, or a professor Fred Millett against a dissenting colleague—and that the younger generation, liberal-minded, should be puzzled by that kind of energy, expended over mere liberalism. Professional liberal leaders are for the most part middle-aged and older men, who grew up under the slogans of Wilsonianism (we fought for democracy), and the New Deal (we fought for freedom from fear). They made their revolution and consolidated their positions, and occupy the influential posts, and have successfully disseminated their ideology. But there is growing up a generation that has not been too busy fighting for liberalism to wonder whether liberalism is worth fighting for. That generation's apathy is traceable not merely to the dilution of spirit that always follows a complete victory. It is a reciprocal infidelity that liberalism itself invites. Liberalism cannot *care* deeply, and so cannot be cared about deeply; and so it leans, altogether, on those whom it has infatuated, who cannot see far enough to see how nearby is the end of liberalism's world. There is nothing there of ultimate meaning to care for, though there is much there to despise. The large majority of students, angled as they are toward liberalism, are silent, reflecting the great emptiness of their faith.

THE LIBERAL—His Root Assumptions

THE CLAIMS FOR DEMOCRACY

> "The people who make the revolution always seem
> to ask for liberty."
> "But do they ever get it, Mr. Gumbril?" Mr. Bojanus
> cocked his head playfully and smiled. "Look at 'istory,
> Mr. Gumbril, look at 'istory. First it's the French Revolu-
> tion. They ask for political liberty. And they gets it. Then
> comes the Reform Bill, then Forty-Eight, then all the
> Franchise Acts and Votes for Women—always more
> and more political liberty. And what's the results, Mr.
> Gumbril? Nothing at all. Who's freer for political liberty?
> Not a soul, Mr. Gumbril. There was never a greater
> swindle 'atched in the 'ole of 'istory. And when you
> think 'ow those poor young men like Shelley talked
> about it—it's pathetic," said Mr. Bojanus, shaking his
> head, "really pathetic."
>
> ALDOUS HUXLEY, Antic Hay.

PROFESSOR RICHARD WEAVER shrewdly observed that
in recent years method has become the reigning absolute.* It used to be that subject matter had precedence
over method. But modish philosophical systems, not-
ably logical positivism, whose rise has coincided with
and to a crucial extent made possible the rise of contemporary liberalism by providing it with its metaphysical base, have effected a revolution. Method is king—
because things are "real" only in proportion as they

_____
* See, e.g., "The Roots of the Liberal Complacency," National Review, June 8, 1957.

99

are discoverable by the scientific method; with the result that method logically directs all intellectual (to which we subordinate moral and metaphysical) traffic.

The consequences of the instrumental view of life and the transfer of attention from subject-matter to method are instantly apparent in various articles of the liberal creed. Our preoccupation these days, as I indicated in the preceding chapter, is not so much with the *kind* of society democracy brings forth in a given political situation, as with democracy itself. We worry about how much academic freedom there is on this campus or that one, rather than about what is being done by the intellect-made-free. The talk is about education as a process, not about the goals of education; indeed we are not permitted to stipulate the goals of education except in methodological terms (education must teach one "how to" think, "how to" adjust, "how to" find happiness, etc.)—because it is heretical to conclude that education can have objective goals. Rather, it is for each student, exercising his Democratically-Guaranteed right of Academic Freedom to employ the Scientific Method to decide what is *his* truth.

Professor Ernest van den Haag, moving from premises very like Weaver's, carries forward his observations to identify a central weakness of the democratic West in its quarrel with Communism.* The secular ideology of liberalism, which sets the tone of contemporary Western thought, is no match for Communism because it is not a redemptive creed. The Communists' program is capable (at least for a period of time, until the illusion wears off) of being wholly satisfactory, emotionally and intellectually, to large numbers of people. The reason for this is that Communist dogma is eschatologically conceived. Communism promises the elimination of poverty, war, inequality, insecurity. Communism offers a view of human history, holds out a millennial vision, indicates the means (revolution) of effecting this millen-

---

* See "Communism, Democracy and Religion," *National Review*, March 22, 1958.

nium. "Where Communism is established," Mr. Van den Haag observes, "this faith functions as opiate; where it is to come, the vision is a powerful stimulant for the dedicated."

Democracy, by contrast, talks a wholly different language. In fact, democracy is nothing more than a procedural device aimed at institutionalizing political liberty. It has no program. It cannot say to its supporters: do thus, and ye shall arrive at the promised land. Far from being capable of defining the millennium, democracy's first commitment is to guarantee that 50 per cent plus one of the people may put an end to any dalliance with a previously acknowledged millennium. Thus it cannot, alone, provide the faith, the opiate, or the stimulant.

Even so, have not the liberals ideologized—having, of course, first idealized—democracy? Is democracy, as Mr. Frank Chodorov said, the last refuge of liberalism? Finding themselves without a program expressible in other gross material terms, have they not attempted alchemical experiments on democracy, transmuting it to the status of the Virtuous Society? Isn't the whole of the liberal ideology agglutinated by semantical raids on substantive ideals?

1.

Let us at any rate concede the confusion with which the term democracy has come to be used. It cannot be denied that, as when Albert Jay Nock first said it, it continues true that "there must be as many different kinds of democracy in this country as there are of Baptists. Every time one of our first-string publicists opens his mouth, a 'democracy' falls out; and every time he shuts it, he bites one in two that was trying to get out." The persistent misuse of the word democracy reflects either an ignorance of its ontological emptiness; or (and is this not the logical derivative of the ignorance?), the pathetic attempt to endow it with substantive meaning.

Consider the semantic pandemonium around "democracy," well illustrated by editorial comment on a single page of the *New York Times* (November 18, 1958). It was a day, clearly, on which democracy, whatever one means by it, was in crisis in different parts of the world. In Ghana, a chaotic situation grew more chaotic as Prime Minister Nkrumah outlawed the opposition. In Venezuela, Admiral Larrazábal, hero of the revolution against Dictator Pérez Jiménez, welcomed, in writing, the support of Venezuelan Communists in his campaign for president. In the Sudan, General Ibrahim Abboud (following the recent examples of Pakistan and Thai) moved in his tanks, ousted the Premier, suspended the constitution, uttered some pomposities, and proceeded to rule. In the American South, the fight over integration moved forward on a number of fronts, and Orval Faubus reiterated his refusal to integrate Little Rock schools.

The *New York Times,* in an editorial, greeted one of the week's developments by laying down a bit of democratic doctrine: "General Abboud . . . has overthrown a *democratic,* parliamentary regime and installed a military dictatorship. This is never a cause for rejoicing." (Several months before, the *Times* had accused General de Gaulle of doing, in effect, the same thing, by refusing to denounce the revolt of the Army in Algeria; and subsequently 80 per cent of the French people democratically confirmed de Gaulle's coup.)

On the same page, the *Times* published a letter from a man in Plainfield, New Jersey: "Could it be that the actions of [Governor Faubus] accurately mirror the wishes *democratically* expressed of most of the people of Arkansas? . . . It seems to me . . . you should inveigh against the people of that sovereign state and not simply against him who does their will."

Another letter, on the same page, written by a professor of political science, deplored the sentencing of Fadhil al-Jamali, by an Iraqi court, to be hanged. "Jamali's real crime is that he believes in Western *democracy* and sought to bring about *democracy* in his own country by such measures as the allocation of 70 per cent of Iraq's huge oil revenues for capital improvements, mainly in education, irrigation and public roads. In condemning him the present Iraqi government . . . is giving an earnest of its contempt for *democratic* leadership and *democratic* ideals."* (My italics, of course.)

Clearly a very large number of the world's problems qualify, by the multiplicity of current definitions, as problems of "democracy." The editors of the *Times* tell us one must *"never"* overthrow an established democratic regime—though they cheered when Perón's regime, which had been democratically voted in, and probably had majority support to the end, was, undemocratically, overthrown by a military junta. Isn't Orval Faubus practicing democracy in Arkansas, a writer asks, and if so what are we democrats crying about? A professor of *political science,* no less, understands democracy to consist in spending money on education, irrigation, and public roads; while the democratic successor to a Venezuelan strongman appeals to Communists for their (democratic?) support.

Clive Bell observed that the grandeur and nobility of the Allied cause (during the first World War) "swelled in ever vaster proportions every time it was restated"—reaching its apogee in our explicitly formulated determination to make the world safe for democracy. The inadequacy of so gross and naive an oversimplification of the national objective is more widely acknowledged today than a generation, or even a decade ago; but even so, Self-Rule continues to tyrannize over the liberal ideology, secure in its place as the *summum bonum.* It follows, of course, that to harbor an undemocratic thought is to be guilty, under the law of liberalism, of the highest form of treason.

The apotheosis of democracy grew out of the euphoria of the nineteenth century. Social philosophy having solemnly concluded that man is essentially and

---

* *"When you question the loyalty of an electrician you are attacking Electricity."*—caption from a recent cartoon by John Kreuttner in *National Review*.

irrepressibly good, infinitely and irresistibly perfectible, it followed naturally that the best government is that most sensitively reflecting the developing refinements in man. There originated in this Couéism of the nineteenth century the reckless stampede to inflate the electoral lists, culminating in the grotesquerie of the State of Georgia, which voted in 1943 to give the vote to every 18-year-old.

The commitment by the liberals to democracy has proved obsessive, even fetishistic. It is part of their larger absorption in Method, and Method is the fleshpot of those who live in metaphysical deserts. Even though democracy is a mere procedure, all the hopes of an epoch were vested in it. Intellectuals have tended to look upon democracy as an extension of the scientific method, as the scientific method applied to social problems. In an age of relativism one tends to look for flexible devices for measuring *this* morning's truth. Such a device is democracy; and indeed, democracy becomes epistemology: democracy will render reliable political truths just as surely as the marketplace sets negotiable economic values.

The democracy of universal suffrage is not a bad form of government; it is simply not necessarily nor inevitably a good form of government. Democracy must be justified by its works, not by doctrinaire affirmations of an intrinsic goodness that no mere method can legitimately lay claim to.

2.

In a period of a few weeks during the fall of 1957, one could observe a significant difference in the attitude of spokesmen for American liberalism toward two political rituals, insignificantly different from one another, taking place in Latin America. In Venezuela, Pérez Jiménez was boss (even though his days were numbered). For the show of the thing, he decided to hold an "election," at which the people (*all* the people, of course) would have the option of "approving" the government of Pérez Jiménez or—well, no one was exactly sure, or what. Indeed, here was a palpable travesty on democracy, and the press of democratic nations took due notice of the fact. There were those who are free of the superstitions of liberalism who joined in denouncing Pérez Jiménez' "election"; for his offense was one of humbuggery, an offense the objection to which cuts across ideological lines.

The Republic of Mexico, on the other hand, observes the forms much more carefully, and for her pains is generally regarded as a member, in good standing, of the democratic family of nations. At just about the time that Pérez Jiménez announced his election, word went out that Adolfo López Mateos was to be nominated by the *Partido Revolucionario Institucional* to succeed President Ruiz Cortines.

Here is how these things proceed in Mexico. Cortines and a few insiders, men generally speaking who have never submitted to public inspection at the polls, decide whom they want as presidential successor, taking into account, to be sure, political realities within their party. P. R. I. is given the word. One sunny day the Brotherhood of Revolutionary Bricklayers (or any other labor union) runs a full page advertisement in all the local dailies, announcing that the will of the revolutionary bricklayers must not be thwarted: the most excellent, most patriotic, most beneficent Adolfo López Mateos (whose name, by the way, was probably not known, at this point, to five thousand Mexicans, and certainly not to many bricklayers) *must* be nominated by P. R. I., to satisfy the people's enlightened cravings. The next day, five other unions run full page ads. The following day two dozen. Meanwhile, painters have started proclaiming the virtues of Don Adolfo López quite literally on the housetops; and on street cars, walls, in bull fight arenas, the name of Adolfo Mateos begins to blossom. By nomination day, Adolfo Mateos' only serious opponent for national attention is Coca Cola. P. R. I. then holds a "democratic," "wide-open" convention. The nation has a "democratic" election campaign, complete with live opposition candidates, and——the will of the people is done.*

P. R. I. has never lost an election (it was founded in 1928) and, I judge, will not lose one except some day way off in the future, and then to a new set of "revolutionaries," who are sure to justify their revolution in the name of democracy. But behold how it pays to observe carefully the ritual of self-rule, not only in external relations, but internally as well. What was the quality of life, under Pérez Jiménez in Venezuela, as compared with life under, say, Miguel Alemán (1946–1952), the most popular president in recent Mexican political history? If democracy is to be defined according to criteria suggested by the professor of political science who wrote to the *Times* protesting the sentencing of Jamali, Pérez Jiménez comes out about as democratic as Alemán, having spent roughly the same percentage of the national income (22 per cent–27 per cent) on federal enterprises. Graft? I do not know how much Pérez Jiménez stole, but very much doubt it exceeded the eight hundred million dollars which one insider estimated as the cost to Mexico of Alemán's six year term.** Life for the average citizen, *Caeteris paribus,* about the same, except that in Venezuela any dissenting political activity was forbidden, whereas in Mexico only meaningful political activity is forbidden. A further and important psychological difference: there was no seeming end to the tenure of Pérez Jiménez. Alemán was confined to a statutory six year term.

There are differences, then. But they are largely differences of form——the kind of difference liberalism must end up concerning itself with, lacking a more profound discriminatory apparatus. I am saying that since democracy is not workable in some nations, at their present

---

* Minority vote in 1958 presidential election: 10 per cent.
** "General Francisco Aguilar of the government party . . . charged that Alemán and his friends drained the country of some $800 million, and laid away $450 million of it in the U.S., Canada, Switzerland and Cuba." *Time,* September 14, 1953. That estimate is high, though not necessarily inaccurate.

stage of development, the liberals, rather than re-examine their categorical assumptions about democracy, come to terms with reality by gladly accepting such subterfuges as are practised in Mexico, India, Indonesia, Ghana, etc.

3.

Self-government does not guarantee the maximization of human freedom. The majority of the people may, indeed often do, by the full exercise of their political privileges, opt to curtail freedom.* A society is not "free" merely because the freedoms the people are doing without are those they voted at the last election to do without. Societies are free according as the people in them are free; the more free the individual, the more free the society. A society ideally free would certainly be self-governed, political freedom being a very important freedom; but *in a free society the people would cherish a self-denying ordinance under which they would never use their political power in such fashion as to diminish the area of human freedom.* That is to say, in an ideally free society, the use of one's political freedom would be highly restricted. That, of course, is the idea behind constitutionalism.

And then political freedom becomes less and less meaningful as political authority is centralized. In America, an individual's vote on a matter of importance

---

* E.g., The views of staunchly self-governing British historian and theorist of social-democracy, E. H. Carr: "The donkey needs to see the stick as well as the carrot . . . I confess that I am less horror-struck than some people at the prospect, which seems to me unavoidable [in England] of an ultimate power, of what is called direction of labor resting in some arm of society, whether in an organ of state or of trade unions." (From *The New Society*, 1951). Or those of P. C. Gordon Walker, former Secretary of State for Commonwealth Relations in the Attlee government: "The new State will also directly augment authority and social pressure by new powers of punishment and compulsion. So far from withering away, as in theory both the individualist and the total State should, the new State, if it is to bring into being and serve the better society, must create new offenses and punish them." (From *Restatement* (!) *of Liberty*, 1951).

has about the weight of a grain of sand.* Effective political freedom yields palpable results. It is the kind of freedom a man enjoys when his voice has a discernible effect on the political determinations by which he is to live. Town-hall democracy is the classical American example. Political freedom is meaningful, I am saying, in proportion as political power is decentralized. The political tendencies of our time are continuingly centralist, and have reached the point generally where it is impossible to infer the extent to which a people are free from the mere fact that they enjoy *political* freedom. In the last analysis, political freedom guarantees freedom only to the collectivity, within which the individual may be enslaved.

What of the presumption that the democratic society is virtuous? What are the hallmarks of the virtuous society? The people must be free, and should live together peaceably, in order, justice and harmony, guided by prescriptive and traditional norms. I see no fixed correlation between the democratic society and the just society; and certainly none between the stable society and the democratic society.

On the contrary, *The Economist,* commenting on the irresponsible behavior of the Labor Party during the spring of 1958, correctly observed that the very existence of British society is jeopardized by the glowering presence of the Labor opposition, with its reiterated threats to undo the government's basic reforms next election day plus one. The very existence of parties that threaten, on coming to power, to annul the contractual commitments of a previous government, has the effect of undermining the power and influence of

---

* To be sure, there is the formidable restraining influence of the negative political power of the people, which could not exist without political liberty. An old man who, over his lifetime, has cast his votes consistently with the socialist third parties, can maintain with plausibility that as far as he is concerned, his democratic birthright turned out to be wholly meaningless to him, never having tasted its fruits by supporting a victorious candidate. The fallacy lies in the fact that the existence of minority parties is likely to affect the policies of victorious parties.

incumbent governments, contributing to social instability. Can a nation with a strong socialist minority ever be stable, when the shadow of socialism renders private property perpetually insecure?

And then, of course, in a revolutionary age there are the revolutionary political parties, whose explicit aim is to overturn the bases of society, and which are no less revolutionary because they seek to revolutionize with the consent of the majority. (I certainly do not suggest that the existence of a Communist minority is good reason for doing away with democracy, though I would say it is sufficient reason for doing away with the Communists.) In a word, democracy does not necessarily provide stability.

Democracy's finest bloom is seen only in its natural habitat, the culturally homogeneous community. There, democracy induces harmony. Harmony (not freedom) is democracy's finest flower. Even a politically unstable society of limited personal freedom can be harmonious if governed democratically, if only because the majority understand themselves to be living in the house that they themselves built. An example is the France of the Fourth Republic, where individual freedoms were appreciably restricted (through inflation, taxation, economic regulation, conscription, etc.), where political instability was the order of the day, where a minority Communist Party often appeared on the verge of bringing the society down—but where social cohesion nevertheless proved possible. To be sure, this may be a tribute to Frenchmen rather than to "democracy." There was no such harmony in Republican Spain.

We see in the revolt of the masses in Africa the mischief of the white man's abstractions: for the West has, by its doctrinaire approval of democracy, deprived itself of the moral base from which to talk back to the apologists of rampant nationalism. The obvious answer to a Colonel Mobutu is: Your people, sir, are not ready to rule themselves. Democracy, to be successful, must be practiced by politically mature people among whom there is a consensus on the meaning of life within their society. We resist your efforts not because we wish to freeze your people in their servile condition, but because we deny the right to which you appeal.

The point remains: the claims that are made in behalf of democracy, the showpiece of the liberal ideology, are illusory, because the attributes imputed to it are wholly extrinsic to democracy itself.

Yet the democratic obsession shapes the liberal's attitude not only in faraway places, like Indonesia, India, and Africa, but here at home.

4.

In the debates that have raged for years and will go on and on, over the civil rights of Negroes in the South, the issue is most concretely joined in the question whether it is the duty of the federal government to guarantee the Negro's access to the ballot. It is well known that in certain quarters in the South where Negroes heavily preponderate, the marginal Negro voter is, by one evasion or another, deprived of the vote. By the marginal Negro voter I mean the man whose vote would tip the scales in favor of the Negro bloc. To deprive him of his vote it becomes necessary, for mechanical reasons, to deprive others like him of their vote, hence what amounts to the virtual disfranchisement of the race in Southern communities that fear rule by a Negro majority. And on those rare occasions when an offending local official is brought to trial, charged with depriving a citizen of his civil rights, he has counted on a jury of local white citizens to deflect the law.

The jury system is, among other things, the mechanism that spans the abstractions by which a society is theoretically guided. The jury is empowered, by its unchallengeable authority, to establish the "fact," and to reconcile the demands of theoretical justice with the complex realities of complex human situations. Trial by jury has the effect of permitting citizens to suspend the application of the law, and juries are known to exercise their authority when they become convinced that there is transcendent reason to interpose between the law and its violator. In parts of the South, the white members of overwhelmingly black communities have shown a resolve to prevail. They mean to prevail on any issue on which there is corporate disagreement between Negro and white; and they appear prepared to take whatever measures are necessary to make certain that they have their way. The most common of these measures is to deprive the marginal Negro of his vote when that vote would be decisive.

The generic question is whether the minority in a democratically organized community is ever entitled to take such measures as are necessary to prevail, politically and culturally, over the majority. It is an ancient question, often confused with the very different question whether dominant minorities are entitled to use their power for the economic exploitation of the majority. The answer to the first question is surely Yes, there are circumstances when the minority can lay claim to preeminent political authority, without bringing down upon its head the moral opprobrium of just men. In the South, the white community is entitled to put forward a claim to prevail politically because, for the time being anyway, the leaders of American civilization are white—as one would certainly expect given their preternatural advantages, of tradition, training, and economic status. It is unpleasant to adduce statistics evidencing the median cultural advancement of white over Negro; but the statistics are there, and are not easily challenged by those who associate together and call for the Advancement of Colored People. There are no scientific grounds for assuming congenital Negro disabilities. The problem is not biological, but cultural and educational. The question the white community faces, then, is whether the claims of civilization (and of culture, community, regime) supersede those of universal suffrage. The British clearly believed they did when they acted to suppress the irruption in Kenya in 1952. There the choice was dramatically one between civilization and barbarism. In the American South there is no such polarity; the matter is one of degree. The white South perceives, for the time being at least, qualitative differences between the level of its culture and the Negroes', and intends to live by its own.

A conservative feels a sympathy for the Southern position which the liberal, applying his ideological abstractions ruthlessly, cannot feel. If the majority wills what is socially atavistic, then to thwart the majority may be the indicated, though concededly the undemocratic, course. It is more important for a community, wherever situated geographically, to affirm and live by civilized standards than to labor at the job of swelling the voting lists. Sometimes it is unfeasible for a minority to have its way; in which case the minority must give ground, and face the fact of social regression—as Argentinians did after Perón won the presidential election. Sometimes the minority cannot prevail except by force; then it must determine whether the prevalence of its will is worth the price of using force—a decision which responsible Argentinians finally, after living under Perón for several years, answered in the affirmative.

The premise of those who argue for implacable legislation to grant every dispossessed Negro the vote is the absolute right of universal suffrage. On this absolute, a towering ideology has been built. But the premise is shaky. Does the vote really make one free? I do not believe it necessarily does, as I have said. Being able to vote is no more to have realized freedom than being able to read is to have realized wisdom. Reasonable limitations upon the vote are not recommended exclusively by tyrants or oligarchs (was Jefferson either?). The problem of the South is not how to get the vote for the Negro, but how to train the Negro—and a great many whites—to cast a thoughtful vote.*

---

* I should like to register an aside. There are two fields in which the Negroes, were they all enfranchised, might be expected to vote as a bloc. The first is education: I should guess they would vote to abolish segregated schools (though I am familiar with the argument that the Negroes approve separate schools). The results of such a vote could cause violent social dislocations. Fearing that, a white

112

The South should prove its bona fides by applying voting qualification tests impartially, to black and white, following the pattern of the State of Alabama, which has drafted pupil placement laws designed to defend the intellectual, moral, and cultural integrity of its schools against the abstract impositions of judicial ideologues. The Southern crisis, growing in tension, may set into motion the first radical reversal of the long drive to universalize the suffrage. Fifty per cent of the people of Southern State X have access to the polling booth, while the fifty per cent who are Negro do not. The drive to extend the suffrage to one hundred per cent has generated countervailing impulses, which may end up reducing the total vote to twenty-five per cent. Among the twenty-five per cent there should certainly be Negroes. The restriction of the vote by such means should allay the Southerners' fear that their society will end. And an organic challenge to the premier premise of liberalism would, of course, have been issued.

It is a pity that there has developed the talismanic view of democracy, as the indispensable and unassailable solvent of the free and virtuous society. It is a pity not only because so much time has been wasted, and blood spilled, in an idolatrous pursuit, but because the usefulness of democracy, which is considerable, is here and there lost from sight. Not so many Americans have downgraded democracy in the wake of our lost illusions about it, but many others have, surveying the great wreckage of two world wars fought for democracy. The

man is moved by respectable consideration to deny the marginal Negro the vote. But even if it is not violence that he fears, the white man is still well motivated so long as his intention is to safeguard intellectual and moral standards which he is convinced stand to be diluted under integration (as, for example, educational standards in Washington, D.C. public schools appear to have been). The second field is economic. The Negroes in the South comprise, generally speaking, the lowest economic class. Given plenipotentiary political power, Negroes would be likely to use it to levy even further (Negro facilities are for the most part paid for by dollars taxed from whites) against the propertied class—which is, by and large, composed of whites. I believe it is man's right to use his political influence to protect his property; but one should be plain about what one is up to, as not all Southerners are.

wreckage is made up of the collapsed surrealisms of the ideologues, who succeeded finally in pushing Couéism right over the cliff. The humbler claims for democracy are not only legitimate, but realistic. It is right that the views of the individual who stands to be affected by a law or ordinance, should be canvassed. It remains only to be added that standards exist by which to appraise the man's views. And that if these views argue for barbarism or regimentation, it is proper to circumvent them, even if, in doing so, democracy is flouted; as it deliberately is under the Constitution of the United States.

In the tense closing hours of the 1958 gubernatorial campaign in New York, Averell Harriman, grown desperate, loosed on his opponent three of the most sinister imaginable political imputations. The first had to do with Nelson Rockefeller's alleged inconstancy to Israel, but quickly backfired when friends of Rockefeller were able to show that he had been giving barrels of money to The United Jewish Appeal dating back even to before Israel existed, perhaps even back to before Mr. Rockefeller contemplated a political career. The second two charges evidently worried Rockefeller so much that he spent virtually all his talking moments, right through to election day, denying he had ever entertained any such heinous thoughts. In no circumstance would he 1) permit a rent rise in rent-controlled New York, nor 2) stand by while the subways raised their fares.

I am tempted to dig out the root economic assumptions of the liberal ideology by examining liberal attitudes toward rent control. There are, however, two reasons why a look at the New York subways is more rewarding. The first is that a discussion of rent control is likely to bring in complications growing out of the non-expansibility of land, complications of the kind Henry George brought into focus. Secondly, in a discussion of the New York subways the old devil-profit is obligingly absent, since the subways belong to the people of the City of New York.

Under its charter, the Transit Authority of New York is required to pay its own way. I do not know the explicit rationale put forward by the authors of this provision, but I should think it easy to guess: namely, that the municipal incorporators saw no conceivable reason why a monopoly catering to several million people per day, a monopoly obliged to pay no taxes and accumulate no profits, a monopoly with the credit of the City of New York available to it when seeking loans for capital improvements—saw no reason why so privileged an enterprise should under any circumstances be allowed to run up an operating deficit, to be made up by outside funds.

Since the war, the price of a subway ride in New York had risen three hundred per cent, from five to fifteen cents. In the fall of 1958, during the New York election campaign, a spokesman for the Transit Authority issued a warning: receipts were once again falling below expenses. More of that, he said, and the subways will have to raise their fares (the alternative of reducing expenses was not alluded to).

Now let us assume that the subways are being managed with peak efficiency (that is, let us forget for the moment the meaning of the history of socialized enterprise), and that the Transit Authority cannot transport four million persons a day around New York at fifteen cents a ride.

Having ruled out economies, what is to be done? The calumny Mr. Harriman attempted to pin on Mr. Rockefeller was that he would permit the Transit Authority to do the only thing the Transit Authority is permitted by law to do, namely, raise the fares. But raising subway fares is politically explosive business, which is why Mr. Rockefeller went to infinite pains to express himself as horrified at the very thought of such a thing. What must be done, both he and Mr. Harriman seemed to agree (first, of course, one must "study" the problem), is to meet the subway deficits out of general funds.

This would mean, of course, a net imposition on non-subway riders, for the benefit of subway riders. If it goes according to plan, some time in the near future Cayuga County apple pickers will be making it possible for Manhattan elevator operators to ride to work for fifteen cents, even though it costs the Transit Authority twenty cents to carry them. In due course, the political representatives of Cayuga apple pickers will appeal, cogently, for increased off-season benefits for apple pickers; whereupon it will become necessary to increase the taxes of subway riders. Keep this up, you will readily see, and the skies are black with crisscrossing dollars. A dispassionate accountant, viewing the purposeless pell mell, would surely wonder what on earth is this all about? It is liberalism on the wing.

What, concretely, is wrong with the economy of the crisscrossing dollar? Well, for one thing there is the well known fact that any time a Cayugan sends a dollar down to New York, it is going to stop at Albany for an expensive night out on the town. (Business expense.) But aside from the leakage, what is awry in a political economy in which dollars are exchanged by political negotiation?

The principal objection is that we have here an economics of illusion, made possible by the systematic mystifications of politicians. The second is that it permits economic profiteering by politically mobilized economic groups at the expense of those not mobilized.* The third is that it diminishes the influence of the individual in the economic marketplace, transferring what the individual loses to politicians and ideologues.

---

* A comment by a professor of economics at Yale University on a speech in New Haven by Walter Reuther (December 1958), reported in the Yale *Daily News*. ". . . there is little danger that either [Reuther's] treatment or most of his figures will be confused with the sum of reality . . . Most conspicuously absent was any facing up to the big issue—the question of how much power any pressure group in a society should have to tilt the economy in its favor at the expense of other groups . . . What is good for the U.A.W.—or G.M.—is not necessarily what is best for America, even if Walter Reuther and Charlie Wilson sing it as a duet. It is not clear, for example, why ill-paid New Haven school teachers should, in effect, have to make a transfer payment to highly paid monopolies of bricklayers or auto workers, in order to enjoy their products."

In the last days of 1958, Senator Jacob Javits of New York sent his constituents a glowing year-end report. From the middle of 1952 through 1958, he wrote, the federal government spent the enormous sum of twenty-eight billion dollars in New York State. The statistic was jubilantly filed, and the Senator further uplifted his constituents by reminding them that the expenditure of "federal funds [in New York] generated additional public and private spending [in] . . . New York."

What was the liberal Senator from New York trying to tell his constituents, if not that New York, thanks to the acumen of its political representatives of whom he has the honor to be one, is getting an out-size slice of the federal pie?

But what did New York contribute to the pie-maker? During the identical period, the federal government received in taxes paid by New York citizens and corporations, $83,600,000,000, or about three times the sum of money that found its way back. Granted the bare statistic is misleading because a substantial amount of the money disbursed by the federal government is not recoverable by any individual state (e.g., foreign aid, all the money spent in the District of Columbia, etc.).

Still, the facts are these: Projecting the figures for the period 1951 to 1956, New York State can be expected to pay 18.5 per cent of future tax levies. The percentage of any federal aid program it is likely to receive, using the same base, is 6.9 per cent. In other words, New York senators and congressmen anxious to spend, say, $100 million of "federal" money on New York education, will find themselves voting to tax New Yorkers about 275 million dollars, to make that possible. By contrast, Mississippi puts up 0.22 per cent of the federal tax dollars—and gets back 2.07 per cent. So that the Mississippi delegation in Congress can assume that for every million dollars of extra taxes he loads down on his fellow Mississippians for federal aid projects, he can return Mississippi 10 million dollars. (Other figures: California pays in 7.4 per cent, gets back 7.7 per cent.

Illinois pays in 8.2 per cent, gets back 4.1 per cent. Montana pays in 0.10 per cent, gets back 0.71 per cent. South Dakota pays in 0.11 per cent, gets back 0.66 per cent.)

The question is, do New Yorkers know what they are up to, in supporting federal aid programs? If they do, it is not because the Javitses of this world have told them.

The evasiveness of liberal economic theory complements the deviousness of their political rhetoric. There is considerable sentiment in New York, for the most part stimulated by liberal organizations, in favor of federal aid to education; indeed, the majority of New York's congressmen voted in favor of the preliminary measure passed by Congress in the summer of 1958.

Now I am convinced there are residents of New York State who are concerned with the depressed level of education in Mississippi to the point of wanting to contribute New York dollars to the advancement of Mississippi education. But I am just as convinced that they do not number one-tenth of one per cent of the population of the state—which, notwithstanding, is on record in the 85th Congress, as I say, as favoring federal aid to education.

The explanation is clear: the average New York voter is simply not aware that the federal government, in order to disburse a couple of billion dollars, will have to collect a couple of billion dollars; that as a resident of one of the wealthiest, per capita, states in the Union, the New Yorker will find himself contributing three times the per capita average, but receiving no more than the average in return; that therefore the net effect of the federal program on the New Yorker is to drain resources from New York State. Federal aid programs are, for New Yorkers, a form of auto-taxation. But the voters do not know this, and Jacob Javits is not going to tell them, any more than Nelson Rockefeller or Averell Harriman did.

Consider a collateral political meaning of federal aid to education. The educational lobby in New York State wants more classrooms built. It appeals to the legislature for them. The legislature turns down the request. The lobby trains its efforts on the federal government, agitating for a federal program. A government that spends six billion on the farmers can surely afford to spend two billion on the children, one legislator booms; and the bill is made law. The cost of the federal program, as it affects the New Yorkers, is far greater than it would have been if Albany had appropriated the money; but that is neither here nor there. The point is that the lobby has got around the New York legislature. The classrooms are being built, the government is paying the cost, New Yorkers are paying the government (at, to be sure, the rate of $1.35 for fifty cents' worth of classroom), the local legislature is relieved of political responsibility for increased expenditures. But, in any case, the education lobby has had its way.

Now avant-garde economists have long since made known their distrust of the marketplace—which, we are told, lacks the kind of transcendent vision that advances civilization. Civilization advances, Justice Oliver Wendell Holmes, Jr. told us, through the expenditure of tax moneys. A view shared by some non-liberals, non-conservatives, e.g. "It goes without saying that only a planned economy can make intelligent use of all a people's strength." * Inferentially, civilization is advanced by the carrying out of political decisions, for it is these that the taxes go to pay for. In his book *The Affluent Society,* John Kenneth Galbraith drives the point all the way home: decisions affecting the disposition of those surplus funds an affluent society can be counted on to generate, must be made by a central authority; by the kind of people who can get around provincial New York legislators. Mr. Galbraith, and other "economists" of the same school (they are really socio-political theorists) who have sought consistently to diminish the influence of the individual in the marketplace, call on a central intelligence, a federal bureauc-

---

* [Hitler's] *Secret Conversations,* New York, Farrar, Straus and Cudahy, 1955, p. 15.

racy guided by the academic aristocracy (the liberal drive to diminish the powers of Congress is complementary) to declare X per cent of our dollars surplus. These dollars are to be spent not by the people, but in the people's behalf; in socially useful ways. Add to this the redistributionist goals of liberalism, and one sees why heavy taxation and heavy spending are indispensable to the operation of liberalism.

From which I draw two generalizations. 1) To the extent it is innocent, liberal economic policy is based on the mystique of the spontaneously generated dollar. (When the subway rider was assured by Nelson Rockefeller that he would not have to pay an extra five cents a day to ride the subway, the subway rider did not assume that in the end the cost to him of that subsidy, by the time negotiations with Cayuga County are completed, would be five cents a day, in this-or-that tax.) 2) To the extent it is not innocent, liberal economic policy seeks to circumvent political obstacles by elongating the distance between the place a dollar is collected, and the place where it is spent—in order to foster illusion "1," and enhance the ideologues' power over the disposition of money, and the direction of society.

2.

Halfway through the second term of Franklin Roosevelt, New Deal braintrusters began to worry about mounting public concern with the soaring national debt. In those days, the size of the debt was on everyone's mind; indeed, Franklin Roosevelt had won a landslide victory in 1932 on a platform that contained the pledge to hack away at a debt which, even under the frugal Mr. Hoover, was thought to have grown to menacing size. At just that moment, an insight came to the rescue. Economists throughout the land were electrified by an alluring theory of debt that had grown out of the new, nationalistic economics of John Maynard Keynes. The ghost of the National Debt was finally laid! To depict the intoxicating political effect of the discovery, the artist of the *Washington Times-Herald* drew for the front page of his paper a memorable cartoon. In the center, seated on a throne, was a jubilant FDR, cigarette tilted almost vertically, grinning from ear to ear. Dancing about him in a circle, hands clasped, his ecstatic braintrusters sang together the magical incantation, the great emancipating formula: "WE OWE IT TO OURSELVES!"

In five talismanic words the planners had disposed of the problem of deficit spending. Anyone, thenceforward, who worried about an increase in the national debt was simply ignorant of a central insight of modern economics: what do we care how much we—the government—owe, so long as we owe it to ourselves?

There is no room in a brief chapter on the root economic assumptions of liberalism for technical commentary on such economic *tours de force* as the one about the national debt. I am drawn to the *Times-Herald's* amusing cartoon, and its symbolic significance. A root assumption of the liberal ideology is that, intellectually, man has come to dominate the economic elements, and that we need only will it, in order to have fair weather all the time. The occasional relapses—for instance the recession of the winter of 1957–1958—are due not so much to absence of economic expertise, as to the inexpertness of Republican technicians. An inexpertness traceable, primarily, to their bewitchment by the antique superstitions.

The accelerability of economic development by force of will (a premise of the Point Four Program) is an article of faith for leading liberal spokesmen. Mr. Walter Reuther is fond of observing that the years 1953–1958 (recognize?) were years of an "under-utilization of productive resources"; that had the rate of growth gone forward "dynamically," the gross national product would have been *"140 billion dollars* higher over this period." Though Mr. Reuther relies heavily on a demonology, he does not take the pains to motivate the desire of "big business," "vested interests," "warmongers," and "reactionary politicians" to depress the level of economic activity—at their own expense. One would think no one would work more assiduously than a businessman to implement Mr. Reuther's economic schemes, were it demonstrable that they would raise the national income as dramatically as Mr. Reuther contends.

The point is that economics—which to be sure has always had an uneasy time of it asserting its autonomy as a social science—has become the pliant servant of ideology. For all one knows, Mr. Reuther seriously believes the implementation of his political program would have the salutary economic consequences he describes. But one thing is sure, that even if the program could be demonstrated *not* to have such economic consequences, Mr. Reuther would not modify his politics, any more than the economic stupidity of the collective farm has modified Mao Tse-tung's enthusiasm for it. If ideology calls for a fifteen billion dollar program of public health, the assumption is that the fifteen billion dollars are there—somewhere. It becomes pettifoggery and obstructionism to maintain that the money is *not* "there" in the sense of being readily available and uncommitted. It is reactionary to insist that to produce the money it becomes necessary either to raise the level of economic production, thus increasing tax revenues, raise existing taxes, or inflate the money into existence. Such demurrals, it is easy to see by examining the rhetoric of the heavy spenders, are inadmissible. *What is important is the public health program.*

The salient economic assumptions of liberalism are socialist. They center around the notion that the economic ass can be driven to Point A most speedily by the judicious use of carrot-and-stick, an approach that supersedes the traditional notion of conservatives and classical liberals that we are not to begin with dealing with asses, and that Point A cannot possibly, in a free society, be presumed to be the desired objective of tens of millions of individual human beings.

The liberal sees no moral problem whatever in divesting the people of that portion of their property necessary to finance the projects certified by ideology as beneficial to the Whole. Mr. J. K. Galbraith wages total war against any putative right of the individual to decide for himself how to allocate his resources. The typical liberal will go to considerable pains to avoid having to say, in as many words, that the people don't know what's good for them (the people are not to be thus affronted); and so the new line is that the people, in expressing themselves at the marketplace, are not expressing their own views, but bending to the will of Madison Avenue. "The conventional wisdom,"* Mr. Galbraith writes, "holds that the community . . . makes a decision as to how much it will devote to its public services . . . [that the] people decide how much of their private income and goods they will surrender in order to have public services of which they are in greater need . . . It will be obvious, however, that this view depends on the notion of independently determined consumer wants . . . But . . . the consumer makes no such choice. He is subject to the forces of advertising and emulation by which production creates its own demand. Advertising operates exclusively, and emulation mainly, . . . on behalf of privately produced goods and services." And then there is the notorious ingratitude of man, toward the nobleman who has the courage to tell him what he really wants. "The scientist or engineer or advertising man who devotes himself to developing a new carburetor, cleanser, or depilatory for which the public recognizes no need and will feel none until an advertising campaign arouses it, is one of the valued members of our society. A politician or a public servant who dreams up a new public service is a wastrel. Few public offenses are more reprehensible."** I do not know the name of, and hence am not in a position to

---

* Definition: That which is thought to be wise by people who disagree with Mr. Galbraith, and isn't. My definition, to be sure, is a paraphrase. For Mr. Galbraith's statement of it, see *The Affluent Society*, Ch. II.
** *Op. cit.*, p. 203 (English edition). Mr. Galbraith is a classic example of the liberal-intellectual who sees himself immersed, head barely above water, in the running seas of Philistia. His thesis is nonsense, of course.

lionize, any carburetor-maker, nor do I know the name of a single maker of depilatories (though I am grateful to them all), and surely all the Henry Fords of history do not command the public adulation of a Franklin Roosevelt. No, Mr. Galbraith, it is more nearly the other way 'round: the scientist who develops a new cleanser is likely to find that there is little he can expect in the way of public recognition; and that the financial gain he thought he was at the very least entitled to has been preempted—somebody got there first, namely, the politician or public servant, who, scoring yet another public success, has just sold the people yet another public service that has to be paid for.

The liberals' answer? Tax, to preserve the "social balance." And take public spending out of the hands of the people. Institutionalize your tax system. To avoid having to make the difficult public case for public expenditures year after year we might devise a "system of taxation which automatically makes a *pro rata* share of increasing income available to public authority for public purposes."*

There once was a moral problem involved in taxation. No longer. On the contrary, it is clear that to the extent morality figures at all in taxation, it is as an affirmative imperative. It is morally *necessary* to take from the rich, not merely to give to the poor. If there were no poor, it would still be necessary to take from the rich, egalitarianism being a primary goal of the liberal ideology. In the past generation the concept of private property metamorphosed from a "right" to an instrumental convenience—a long journey from when Aristotle listed "possession" as the tenth "predicament" of the human being. "Probably majority opinion agrees with our own national policy," writes the author of a widely used Freshman economics text about the corollary of private property, freedom of enterprise, "that the right of a man to engage in business for himself is not a basic freedom,

_____
* *Ibid*, p. 243.

124

like freedom from fear [!], and want [!], freedom of speech and of worship."*

And so the way is cleared to set up the problem: Either the individual disposes of his surplus funds—in which case you have stagnation, chaos, dissipation, incoherence, synthesized desires; or else a central intelligence disposes of it—in which case you have order, progress, social balance, coherence. Looked at in this way, the problem ceases to be "Can the people afford to look after their own health, build their own schools, buy their own homes?" and becomes "Does it not make more sense for political governors to allocate the people's resources as between doctors, schools, and homes, to impose order upon the chaotic and capricious allocation of dollars when left to their owners to spend?"

It is not easy to understand the liberals' fear, manifested at so many levels, most recently and most conspicuously in the concerted liberal opposition to right-to-work laws in the individual states, of the voluntary approach to society. Their case is not built on the administrative need for one-hundred per cent cooperation. It does not matter that a program of federal social security might work just as well if enrollment in it were voluntary. If it *were* voluntary, a presumptive majority would still subscribe (I say that because a law that is on the books in a democratic society is presumed to have the majority's support); and, that being so, the secession of a minority would not alter the economic balances the program presupposes.

But as with joining a union, membership must be compulsory. The reasons are sometimes given that the individual cannot be trusted to set aside savings toward his old age, and a government cannot very well address the delinquent, arriving, destitute, at old age, as the ant addressed the grasshopper, refusing him sustenance in the name of abstract justice. But has any liberal sug-

---

* Theodore Morgan, *Income and Employment*, New York, Prentice Hall, 1947, p. 175.

125

gested that in deference to the ideal of free choice an individual be exempted from membership in the social security program if he *has* taken substitute measures to look after his old age, through the use of private pension schemes, investment or insurance programs?

Although they represent only ten per cent of the whole, and are constantly defending themselves against the attacks of secularists and levellers, the private grammar and secondary schools in this country flourish, and operate under the voluntarist dispensation. "Education" is compulsory. Educational facilities are publicly provided. But those who elect to do so, and can afford to, may seek out private educational facilities. The arrangement is a very ancient one, and is secured by the prescriptive sanction of the public. But private schools remain an anomaly of the planned society; they are "divisive" and "undemocratic," in the words of Dr. James Conant, who spoke in 1951 as president of the most venerable private educational institution in the land, and so are subject to indirect and direct harassments. The former consist primarily in steeply progressive income taxes. The latter in such measures as educational anti-discrimination laws, and petty refusals to provide milk and buses, under the pretext that to do so would make the authors of the First Amendment roll about in their graves. "The American people are so enamored of equality," Tocqueville wrote, "that they would rather be equal in slavery than unequal in freedom."

The call by liberalism to conformity with its economic dispensations does not grow out of the economic requirements of modern life; but rather out of liberalism's total appetite for power. The root assumptions of liberal economic theory are that there is no serious economic problem; that in any case economic considerations cannot be permitted to stand in the way of "progress"; that, economically speaking, the people are merely gatherers of money which it is the right and duty of a central intelligence to distribute.

THE IDEA OF LIBERALISM

I have resolved not to read another history of liberalism unless my mother undertakes to write one. I do not think, after a point, one learns very much from them; or, rather, I think one learns, on reaching a certain point, that one does not learn very much from them. If the book is written by a liberal (as they mostly are), liberalism will emerge as consistent and consistently unobjectionable, no matter when one looks at it, whether at the moment when "liberalism" is calling for opposition to the growth of state power, or when "liberalism" is calling for the state's aggrandizement.

For example, Professor J. Salwyn Schapiro, in his *Liberalism: Its Meaning and History** writes, "Laissez faire, a revolutionary doctrine in the eighteenth century, a liberal one in the nineteenth, was repudiated [by liberals] as a reactionary one in the twentieth"; and in each case, the "liberal" was dead on target.

Mr. Schapiro goes on: "The old liberalism had concerned itself mainly with the protection of the individual against arbitrary acts of government. The new liberalism sought to protect him against arbitrary acts of private organizations as well. [*Arbitrary? Do we understand the professor correctly? E.g., when the people decline to eat six loaves of bread a day, even though that many are being produced, the government purchases the uneaten five out of federal funds. To protect the wheat farmers against the people's arbitrariness?*] The newest liberalism [*Mirror, mirror on the wall/Am I the newest of them all?*] found international expression in a resounding [*where on earth has it resounded? Seriously. Where?*] proclamation of both the old and new Rights of Man [*Samples: 'The right of everyone to take part in cultural life,' 'the right to . . . social wellbeing'*] issued by the United Natons . . . in 1948. . . . An ideal of social liberalism was now proclaimed for all mankind by a world body. [*With the support—yes, the USSR signed*

---

* D. Van Nostrand, New York, 1958.

up—of representatives of 600 million slaves] [In 1923] the Laborites [the socialist party of Great Britain] headed by J. Ramsay MacDonald, were truly liberal in their political philosophy . . . It comprehended a critical attitude toward authority, both secular and religious [*How can a political philosophy comprehend a critical attitude toward the secular authority and call, as the English socialists consistently have done, for an infinite multiplication of regulations, enforced by the authority of the state?*], a constant effort to improve living conditions gradually and peacefully [*Why so gradually? Demonstrably it is under* anti-*socialist,* anti-*liberal 'capitalism' that living conditions improve markedly. Why is that wrong? Why wrong if they improve dramatically, as in postwar capitalist West Germany, rather than 'gradually,' as in liberal-socialist England?*] and a generous view of the capacity of the lower classes to rise to higher standards, both moral and intellectual [*'Generous?' As distinct from 'realistic?' Or does the professor mean 'optimistic?' Has the moral caliber of the lower classes—or of the upper classes—risen in a century of liberalism-Liberalism? And what of intellectual standards, have they risen? And if neither the one nor the other has, do we recast our ideas, and thereby become—well, what? 'Parsimonious?' 'Misanthropic?' 'Reactionary?'—'Rationalist?'*]. The recognition of the autonomy of the individual is the very keystone of liberalism. [*Enough! Do you mean the* primacy *of the individual? But that, properly defined, is the keystone of religion, and liberalism is militantly secular, you tell us. 'Autonomous' in the dictionary-sense of 'independent of the whole'? But liberalism is egalitarian, and egalitarianism precludes independence of the whole. No Attican was 'independent' of the length of Procrustes' Bed. What if in the course of exercising his independence, the individual tells the tax collector to go stuff social security into his back pocket? Is he to be left 'autonomous' to do so? Was there ever a social system, this side of doctrinaire Marxism, that dealt, where the individual is concerned, in rounder human numbers than liberalism*

128

does? The only autonomy liberalism appears to encourage is moral and intellectual autonomy; solipsism. And that is the autonomy of deracination; the philosophy that has peopled the earth with atomized and presumptuous social careerists diseased with hubris; the pestilence that breeds those 'squalid oligarchs who detest the world of silence and of freedom' whom, Russell Kirk charges conservatives, it has fallen to us 'to keep at bay.']"

I do not understand liberalism as a historical continuum. I refuse to submit to the facile expositions of liberal historians who do not shrink from coopting for the liberal position any popular hero out of the past. Thomas Jefferson, a liberal when he lived, would be a "liberal" were he alive today because, so their argument goes, the principles he then propounded, *mutatis mutandis,* have evolutionized into the principles of the contemporary liberal. Thomas Jefferson, the humane, ascetic, orderly patrician, countenance the mobocratic approach to belly-government of Harry Truman and the Americans for Democratic Action? But why? What has befallen us, that liberalism should be, ineluctably, the only approach to democratic government, mid-twentieth century? And if what has befallen us is a historical imperative with which we must necessarily come to terms, must we do so joyfully, even to the sacrilegious point of arrogating for it the enthusiasm of Thomas Jefferson? It may be that as James Stephens wrote, "the waters are out and no human force can turn them back"; but is it necessary, he wondered, that "as we go with the stream, we . . . sing Hallelujah to the river god"?

I think it a pity to play along with tendentious historiographers, who find it a workaday challenge to their ingenuity to relate linearly the liberalism of Alexander Hamilton and that of Harold Laski; and so I have not— because truthfully I cannot—treated contemporary liberalism except as a contemporary phenomenon. It is as a contemporary phenomenon that it needs probing, so that we may lay bare its root assumptions. It can be grandly contended that the reason Joseph L. Rauh, Jr. opposed the Jenner-Butler bill to curb the Supreme Court is that once upon a time Montesquieu (who crystallized the idea of the division of government power) dropped a pebble in a pond, whose distant agitation now directs the liberal bark on its present course. I say the liberals, whose disregard for the balance of government power is evidenced by their ruthless drive for aggrandizement of the executive, opposed the bill because they are in the clutch of an ideology that lusts passionately after its proximate objectives, toward the realization of which Mr. Warren's Supreme Court happens to be laboring as an institutional fifth column. We are not, under the circumstances, to Tamper with the Judiciary —not so long as it is headed by men of congenial ideological disposition. If I may, I shall proceed to regard contemporary American liberalism—whatever the waters are that fed it, wherever the fateful point at which they came madly together—as a contemporary phenomenon, of distinctive attributes: the reigning secular ideology of the West.

1.

I have made much of the liberals' obsession with method, having remarked their fetishistic involvement with democracy. The obsession is most clearly discernible in liberal education theories. At last there is widespread public and even intellectual concern over the hegemony of the instrumentalists over primary and secondary education; and in the important Council on Basic Education, liberals have joined with conservatives in resisting the highly organized drive of the educationists to abolish learning. In New York State opponents of progressive education, through a petition to the educational authorities in Albany, have boldly urged that existing regulations be modified to provide that the curricula of the teachers colleges demand of prospective teachers of physics that they devote as many hours to the study of physics as to techniques of teaching! This is to have come a long way, in the march back from the desolation to which the disciples of John Dewey had led us. The penetrating and galvanizing efforts of such cogent critics of modern education as Mortimer Smith, Arthur Bestor, and Russell Kirk have borne fruit; and now *Time,* Inc. is on our side, so the country cannot presume to be far behind.

The seeds of progressive education bear immediate and grotesque fruit. When twenty high school graduates applying for the job of postman are disqualified because they do not know the alphabet, the community is driven to look for the villain, and Messrs. Kirk *et al.* are there to tell them where the villain is holding forth. The deadly fruit of the central and most pernicious feature of liberal educational theory is not so readily spotted, and hence not so quickly spewed out. I speak of the theory of academic freedom.

Academic freedom calls for relieving the scholar of worldly and dogmatic impositions, thereby easing his way to the apprehension of new truths. So far so good; we are dealing indisputably with methods conducive to the advancement of many kinds of knowledge.

But when one asks, What is the purpose of discovering these new truths, and to what purpose have we discovered those truths we now know, there is a riot of confusion. Among the appropriate questions one directs to theorists of academic freedom: 1) Is the apprehended truth true only for the discoverer, or true for everyone else as well? Granted there are the two kinds of truths, should we not here deal only with the latter kind?—because 2) If the community makes positive provisions to encourage an individual scholar to search out truths, is the community not entitled to expect that the scholar's concerns shall be more than subjectively important, that the scholar, if successful, will contribute to the intellectual or moral or scientific patrimony? If so, 3) What is the purpose of discovering a truth, if that truth is not in some way actionable? And does not acting upon that truth require the dislodgement of that which heretofore posed as truth? But 4) Academic communities are prohibited by the theoretical restrictions that derive from academic freedom from taking corporate positions as regards substantive truths. They are therefore helpless when confronted with the question, *What are the consequences of finding those truths the search for which is held to be the principal justification for academic freedom?*

The answers are garbled, but boil down to what one might expect in an age of liberal emphasis. What turns out to be important is not the truths themselves, but the blasted *search* for them! The story of Democracy, all over again. There is the tale (I think it was Ring Lardner's) of the old prospector who labored a lifetime, and one day comes upon a rich deposit of gold. Face to face with what he has been looking for through the years, he puzzles as to what to do with it. He shrinks from the attendant complexities and unpleasantness of mining and monetizing it. On reflection he turns away from his discovery, and goes back to what he is used to doing: prospecting. But he does not work so diligently as before. He is haunted by the fear of another strike, and a repetition of the unsettling experience.

Professor Willmoore Kendall of Yale strikingly epitomized the prevailing theory of higher education. It is based, he said, on "the asymptotic approach to truth." An asymptote is a line toward which the curve on all those familiar graphs bends, but which the curve, while getting closer and closer to it, never quite touches.* Asymptotes, by definition, cannot meet their complementary curves; as, by definition, higher academic inquiry cannot comprehend truth; because to do so presupposes its existence, and raises the disintegrative question, How do we handle it?

Even so, the exhortations to go truth-seeking are deafening. They are perfectly intelligible when the quest is for a cancer cure, or some such thing—but it is not over the cancer-hunters that the fusses involving aca-

---

* A more technical definition: "A line that is the limiting position which the tangent to a curve approaches, as the point of contact recedes indefinitely along an infinite branch of the curve."

demic freedom are made. Other truths than scientific and methodological ones have no objective existence, the liberals in effect contend, and therefore cannot, under the liberal epistemology, be apprehended. Hence the built-in safety of all the injunctions having to do with truth, in baccalaureate rhetoric whose grandiosity is intended primarily for the ears of laymen who must from time to time be reminded to keep their grubby little hands off professional academic business. As for the young scholars, they know, in their hearts, that the exhortation nowadays reduces to *"Ye shall seek the truth as though it existed; and in the seeking of it, ye shall be made free."* As free as the man with the vote is free; free in virtue of having the vote. And never mind if he is free to do anything *other* than go to the polls.

The conservative emphasis is different. Conservatives do not deny the existence of undiscovered truths, but they make a critical assumption, which is that those truths that have *already* been apprehended are more important to cultivate than those undisclosed ones close to the liberal grasp only in the sense that the fruit was close to Tantalus, yet around whose existence virtually the whole of modern academic theory revolves. Conservatism is the tacit acknowledgement that all that is finally important in human experience is behind us; that the crucial explorations have been undertaken, and that it is given to man to know what are the great truths that emerged from them. Whatever is to come cannot outweigh the importance to man of what has gone before.

There is nothing so ironic as the nihilist or relativist (or the believer in the kind of academic freedom that postulates the equality of ideas) who complains of the anti-intellectualism of American conservatives. Such is *our* respect for the human mind that we pay it the supreme honor: we credit it with having arrived at certain great conclusions. We believe that millenniums of intellection have served an objective purpose. Certain problems have been disposed of. Certain questions are closed: and with reference to that fact the conservative orders his life and, to the extent he is called upon by

133

circumstances to do so, the life of the community. Burke said it all, definitively, as ever, when he wrote, "We know that *we* [i.e., Burke and his contemporaries] have made no discoveries; and we think that no discoveries are to be made, in morality; nor many in the great principles of government, nor in the idea of liberty, which were understood long before we were born, altogether as well as they will be after the grave has heaped its mould upon our presumption, and the silent tomb shall have imposed its law on our pert loquacity."

<h2 style="text-align:center">2.</h2>

What is the liberal millennium? So far as I can make out, it is the state in which a citizen divides his day equally between pulling levers in voting booths (Voting for what? It does not matter; what matters is that he vote); writing dissenting letters to the newspapers (Dissenting from what? It does not matter; just so he dissents); and eating (Eating what? It does not matter, though one should wash the food down with fluoridated water).

The liberal ideology is putatively based on the maximization of choice at every level. What is important to the liberal, again putatively, is that there be choice; whereas to the conservative, what is important is, What choices will man, whose first choice was so catastrophic, go on making? In actual practice, the choices, under applied liberalism, are limited by the pressures of an overarching and highly repressive conformity. In the economic sphere, with the ascendancy of Regulation, there came, necessarily, the decline of the voluntary approach to life; and choice was accordingly restricted. In academic life, one is to be unhampered, free to choose. *But one may never choose.* Or, rather, any choice one makes is, by postulate, consigned to eternal insignificance. If I am told I am free to choose between a hamburger and a cheese sandwich, I do not feel my freedom has become fully meaningful until I sink my teeth into one or the other. If I am "free" to pursue the truth, I do not feel that freedom has become fully meaningful unless we stipulate that truths exist, and are apprehensible.

The liberal ideology cannot develop beyond its present point so long as its root delusion is that method is substance. But develop it must; it cannot stand still, for it is "in loss of an object." "The will flags," Russell Kirk observes, "when it no longer perceives any end, any object in existence." Liberalism cannot sustain our civilization on the little it has to offer. It is sustaining the majority of our intellectuals, but that proves to be easier than holding together the world.

II
THE CONSERVATIVE
ALTERNATIVE

The Failure of the Conservative Demonstration

WHEN LORD KEYNES BRUSHED aside the demurrals of a critic concerned with the long run effect of his program by saying "In the long run we are all dead," he originated a verbal fillip that made its way quickly into the annals of definitive retort.* The characteristic political concern of liberalism is for the here and now notwithstanding the rhetorical abstractions about the millennium. The liberal is more at home with revolutions per minute than historical cycles, measuring supersonic thrusts more accurately than glacial advances; and as one might expect in a secularist who lacks a sense of participation in a transcendent process, he is seized by a complementary impatience for immediate results. Leaving aside the question *whether* the Keynesian formula could bring about the advertised economic result, Lord Keynes' point was dialectically self-contained: *if* he could bring about, by his razzle-dazzle economics, the desired economic result, the putative injuries to the long term are worth worrying about only as one worries, in moments of morbid vanity, about whether one's grave will be kept green.

Lord Keynes was facetious about the long term, but the success of his riposte was due in large part to the undoubted fact that conservatives have cheapened the

---

* It is not relevant that in the context in which Keynes first used the crack, he used it with justification. It became the motto of his evangelists, and has been widely used, in the sense in which I use it, to ridicule the critics of the Keynesian school.

vocabulary of caution—by defying the rhetorical maxim that one does not cry "Wolf!" every day, and expect the community to heed one's cries the day the wolf actually materializes. It is not safe to bank on the hearer's perception of genuine distress. If one is on record as reiterating the prediction that the social security law will bring slavery to America in our time, after a while one's warnings will be automatically discounted.

Conservatives, as a minority, must learn to agonize more meticulously. We cannot expect the rhetorical license enjoyed by the liberals, who, as we have seen, are infinitely patient with one another. Senator Paul Douglas, a professionally trained economist and sometime professor of the subject, can harangue the voters of Illinois, as he did in 1954 while campaigning for reelection, with dire talk of impending mass poverty ensuing upon the misanthropic stewardship of a Republican administration. But when years go by and that poverty fails to materialize, he is not brought to account, nor are his credentials as an economist publicly reviewed. The liberals can proclaim a reign of terror, promulgated by Senator McCarthy and Roy Cohn, and be taken seriously the world over. Then, after a while, it is generally agreed that the reign of terror has terminated. We look about, eager to enjoy our manumission—only to find that life is about as it was before; whereupon one's instinct is to call into question whether that reign of terror ever existed. Such a question could precipitate a crisis of confidence between the people and the overlords of opinion who deceived them; so it does not get asked.

We conservatives, on the other hand, are not allowed to forget the direness of *our* predictions. And indeed if we permit ourselves to go on saying the same things about the imminence of catastrophe—if we become identified with the point of view that the social security laws toll the knell of our departed freedoms, or that national bankruptcy will take place the month after next —we will, like the Seventh Day Adventists who close down the curtain of the world every season or so, lose our credit at the bar of public opinion, or be dismissed as cultists of a terrestrial mystique. The conservative demonstration, at the hands of the old guard, has not been made successfully, in part because of the exaggerated pessimism I speak of, in part because conservatism was made to sound by its enemies, frequently with the aid of its friends, like a crassly materialist position, unconcerned except with the world of getting and spending.

On the other hand the new conservatives, many of whom go by the name of Modern Republicans, have not been very helpful. Their sin consists in permitting so many accretions, modifications, emendations, maculations, and qualifications that the original thing quite recedes from view. The conservative movement in America has got to put its theoretical house in order. A day-to-day conservatism of expediency will only carry us from day to day, hazardously, at best. Its vulnerability is as famous as the 1958 elections. Such is the brand of conservatism of Mr. Arthur Larson, advanced with verve and spirit in *A Republican Looks at His Party,** a book that had the singular distinction of being read by President Eisenhower.

That kind of conservatism is dead, coroners of the 1958 general election were agreed, and indeed deserves to be dead, along with any political philosophy based primarily on the radiance of a single political figure. Professor Larson went far—from Under Secretary of Labor to principal speechwriter for the President and director of the U. S. Information Service—in recognition of his uncanny powers of externalizing the meaning of Modern Republicanism. He even contended that Modern Republicanism has a philosophical and political life of its very own, of which Mr. Eisenhower, as President, was merely the embodiment. Today, on mature reflection, Mr. Larson fleshes out the theory of his conservative society, and permits Mr. Eisenhower to blend into the landscape.

In his book,** Professor Larson bases his philosophy

* New York: Harper & Brothers, 1956.
** *What We Are For,* New York, Harpers, 1959, p. 45.

of government on Abraham Lincoln's classically pragmatic remark to the effect that the function of government is to do for the people what needs to be done, but what they cannot do at all for themselves, or so well. However, sensing perhaps that the maxim of Mr. Lincoln does not tell us very much and would be equally acceptable to Mr. Norman Thomas and General Rafael Trujillo, Mr. Larson proceeds to reduce his philosophy of government to mathematical terms. Thus, "$T = E + P$," i.e., "Tyranny Equals Economic Plus Political Power." Fifty-five pages later he repeats the formula in order to hunt down its corollary, to wit, "$F = E' + P'$," i.e., "Individual Freedom Equals Economic Rights Plus Political Rights." Now by such methods one can lend the glamor of scientific exactitude to any political slogan; it becomes a matter, simply, of capitalizing the first letters and supplying an equal sign somewhere along the line (E.g., $F = F \times F'$—Freedom Equals Freedom from Fear Itself.)

In a word, Mr. Larson has a hard time schematizing his political philosophy. This in itself does not condemn his philosophy, but does suggest the difficulty conservatives have had in distilling theoretical guidance out of the kind of Republicanism that was recently in vogue. Not only have the old guard conservatives failed in making the demonstration successfully, the Moderns also have failed. Not only by failing to come up with useful definitions, but by failing to take advantage of their strategic opportunity, while occupying the center of the stage, to direct the attention of the nation to the solid advantages to be got from turning back the clock, as it was turned back, so profitably, by Abraham Lincoln when he freed the slaves, by England when she repudiated socialism after seven years of it, by West Germany when, in 1948, she decided to get out of the way of the marketplace.

Our domestic political engagements are not fought, for the most part, with Communists, none of whose premises we share, but with liberals, with whom we share some. The pragmatic directive of Mr. Lincoln would not suit Communist ideas of history or dogma, but there is nothing there, as I say, that will separate the liberal from the Modern Republican. That being so, it is simply not useful as a philosophy of government distinctive to a single faction in American political life. There is plenty of a programmatic kind that Mr. Larson believes in and the majority of liberals do not. For example, he believes that medicine should not be socialized; but search in his two books though I have, I cannot find any theoretical crossroad at which Mr. Larson and the liberal branch off into opposing camps on the question of nationalized medicine. Certainly not at the point where he quotes Lincoln. Who says government cannot look after the health of the people "better" than they can themselves? Conservatives say so, liberals tend to disagree. Shouldn't the two forces advance theoretical directives that reflect the divergence?

2.

I make the point with some emphasis because the failure of the conservative demonstration is not traceable merely to the rhetorical extravagances of what is known as the extreme right, but also the theoretical insufficiency of the "moderates." The most irrepressible illustration of this has been bequeathed to us by the man for whom Mr. Larson served as philosophical mentor for three years. There is no better illustration, that I know of, and certainly none more galling, of the derivative helplessness of those who lean on such formulas as Mr. Larson's.*

In response to a question at his press conference in late July 1957 as to whether he was considering extending an invitation to Marshal Zhukov to come to America (the Marshal, at the time, had not quite yet been purged), President Eisenhower was prompted to remi-

---

* The confusion I speak of was experienced by Mr. Eisenhower in 1945, long before he knew Mr. Larson. But the confusion in Mr. Eisenhower's mind had not dissipated by 1957, long after he had met Mr. Larson.

nisce about ideological conversations he had had with the Marshal shortly after the end of the war. Mr. Eisenhower's account left one limp with gratitude that ours is not an age in which disputes between nations are adjudicated by forensic contests between heads of state. For in such a contest the champion of the West (the American people had recently—1956—spoken in thundering terms) would be Dwight Eisenhower. And Dwight Eisenhower—prime evidence of the failure of conservatives to make their demonstration—clearly did not know what he was defending, how to defend what he defended, or even whether what he defended was defensible.

Listening to Marshal Zhukov elaborate the virtues of Communism, said the President, he found himself "very hard put to it" to confute him. Marshal Zhukov told the General that the Communist system is an "idealistic" system—unlike capitalism which is "materialistic." Faced with that show of force, the victor over the armies of fascism conceded defeat. "I had a very tough time," he said to the press, "trying to defend our position." *

Mr. Eisenhower, alas, did not mean to say that *he* uniquely—owing to unique personal or intellectual shortcomings, or the unique skill of his adversary, or the unique circumstances that militated against success— was incapable of defending the idealistic pretensions of

---

* EDWARD P. MORGAN, American Broadcasting Company: *Mr. President, . . . would you consider sometime in the future inviting [Marshal Zhukov] to the United States?*
THE PRESIDENT: . . . during the years that I knew [Marshal Zhukov] I had a most satisfactory acquaintanceship and friendship with him. I think he was a confirmed Communist. . . . We tried each to explain to the other just what our systems meant, to the individual, and I was very hard put to it when he insisted that their system appealed to the idealistic, and we completely to the materialistic, and I had a very tough time trying to defend our position, because he said:

"You tell a person he can do as he pleases, he can act as he pleases, he can do anything. Everything that is selfish in man you appeal to him, and we tell him that he must sacrifice for the state." He said, "We have a very hard program to sell." So what I am getting at is, I believe he was very honestly convinced of the soundness of their doctrine and was an honest man. . . .

144

the West. Mr. Eisenhower did not hold *himself* responsible for the lost debate with Mr. Zhukov. He held the West responsible. He did not mean that *he* had difficulty defending the West because of its materialism: he meant that the West is difficult to defend when up against the idealistic claims of Communism.

The attentive and history-minded Mr. James Reston of the *New York Times* rushed to the rescue. Surely, Mr. President, he said, you do not mean to leave us with the impression that liberal democracy is harder to defend than Communism? To which the President, in a classic flight of intellectual disorder,* replied—but to interpret his answer is presumptuous. It defies authoritative paraphrase. Suffice it to say that there was no objective relief there for Mr. Reston, or for the West.

It is a lightly guarded national secret that Mr. Eisenhower has a way of easing virtually every subject he touches into a syntactical jungle in which every ray of light, every breath of air, is choked out. But disadvantageous though this incapacity is (in an age where, War being Unthinkable, so many battles depend on verbal trenchancy), it is not a cause of national alarm. The nation had inarticulate presidents before and, in the short term, survived them. The distinctive danger in the

---

* JAMES RESTON, *New York Times: Do you want to leave the inference that it is difficult to defend the proposition that democracy is a more idealistic system than Communism?*
THE PRESIDENT: Well, I said this: I said when you are talking with the Communists you find it is a little difficult, for the simple reason that you say a man can earn what he pleases, save what he pleases, buy what he pleases with that. Now, I believe this, because I believe in the power for good of the, you might say, the integrated forces developed by 170,000,000 free people. But he said that "We say to the man 'You can't have those things. You have to give them to the state,'" and this is idealistic because they ask these people to believe that their greatest satisfaction in life is in sacrificing for the state, giving to the state. In other words, he takes the attitude that they don't force this contribution, they are teaching a people to support that contribution. So, when you run up against that kind of thing . . . I think you could run into people you could have a hard time convincing that the sun is hot and the earth is round. I don't say that I don't believe it. I am merely saying that against that kind of a belief you run against arguments that almost leave you breathless, you don't know how to meet them.

145

case of Mr. Eisenhower lay in the fact that his inarticulateness was traceable to an organic ignorance of the nature of the society whose well-being it was his historic destiny to watch over at the moment of our great peril. That ignorance, that lack of vision, rendered him, and through him us, relatively impotent at the hands of the Zhukovs. Communism is *not* idealistic and for the most part does *not* appeal to idealistic people; our position, adequately defined, is *not* materialist, and is *not* "hard to defend," and is *not* burdened by a primary appeal to the "selfish in man"; and Marshal Zhukov, whose "idealism" and "honesty" had recently led him to torture and kill a great many aggressively non-idealistic Hungarians, *cannot* be seduced by copybook homilies. He has other things on his mind, i.e., conquering a world whose leaders do not appear able to state convincingly why it is worth the extraordinary exactions required to defend it.

The distinctive challenge of our time, against which Mr. Eisenhower's forty-five-billion-dollar defense budget and Mr. Arthur Larson's books were powerless, is to resist the philosophical infiltration of the West by Communism. That infiltration is the end toward which the great engines of history are busily working, the grand synthesis whose name, in one of its phases, is Coexistence, and whose meaning, for the West, is death. The only defense of the West against it is the tenderest solicitude for Western values, the fastidious cultivation of the Western position, so sorely ravaged by the imprecisions and tergiversations of the leaders of the West. Liberalism cannot teach Mr. Eisenhower to talk back effectively to Mr. Khrushchev; but conservatism can, and hence the very urgent need to make the conservative demonstration.

3.

Before conservatives arrive at the point where it is appropriate to deal in grandiose asseverations, they must face up to homely analytical chores.

146

What do I mean when I say the conservative has tended to speak extravagantly, and has failed to make distinctions?

Let us consider, in some detail, what was once the heated question of the social security laws, which remain the symbol of the welfare state. I say the social security laws were "once" controversial because, as a matter of political reality, they are controversial no longer. (I doubt whether a dozen congressmen would vote today to set the law aside.) But the law remains controversial academically, for the reason that economists and political scientists of eminence, although a small minority in their own professions, are outspokenly opposed to them on several grounds, as are the beleaguered but active libertarians. With these figures a conservative political movement, if it is to be viable, must come to terms, or else suffer the fate of Modern Republicanism, whose historical destiny it was to stay a radical impulse or two for a year or two, in exchange for a considerable erosion of the conservative position.

There are two generic grounds for disapproving federal social security—one economic, the other philosophical.

Let us take the trouble to break down the economic argument. It is widely known that social security deposits are not segregated against future withdrawals, but deposited with common funds that go to meet general government expenses. The economic "idea" behind social security is that at some date in the future, as much money will be flowing into the Treasury in payments by subscribers to social security as will leave the Treasury to meet matured obligations. Now the fact that in its administration of the funds the government does not meet orthodox fiduciary standards of the kind stipulated by the laws of most of the states for private insurance companies, seems to me to be wholly irrelevant. If the Travelers Insurance Company of Hartford, Connecticut, had at its disposal the resources, material and coercive, of the federal government, it is not likely that the legislatures would have troubled to define any further safeguards for the depositors.

The more serious economic case against the federal social security program is based on the certitude of inflation. Given inflation, social security payments would seem to amount, at least in part, to a capital levy, since the dollar paid in when one is twenty-five years old is due to be repaid, forty years later, with a dollar worth only a part of what the original dollar was worth.

But surely it is clear that the value of social security payments is *politically* secured. As inflation depreciates the dollar, so political pressure will require social security payments to increase, to make up for the dollar's depreciated purchased power. To be sure, there is no statutory guarantee that this will happen; but neither is there a guarantee behind the value of the policy taken out with a private insurance company, which is subject to the depredations of inflation unmitigated by meliorative political pressure.

Is federal social security, inflation aside, partially gratuitous in the light of the fact that the assured is paying, or so it appears, a mere one-half of the social security payment, the balance being furnished by his employer? No. That is demagogic hocus-pocus; because the employer classifies his share of the social security payment as a cost-of-labor, pure and simple; and if he were relieved of the obligation to match his employee's payments, he would not profit: the money would go either to the employee in increased wages, or to the consumer in lower prices. Employer participation is merely a form of economic circumlocution, of the kind liberalism relies upon so heavily.

Let us concede that it is unlikely that at any time in the future the income of the social security fund will match its disbursements,* and that the difference will be made up by the government. The net economic cost of the program, then, takes the form of a direct govern-

---

* In fiscal 1957, there was a deficit (for the first time) of 130 million dollars.

ment subsidy. A subsidy in a class with, say, payments to farmers for commodities unmarketable at parity prices. Properly speaking, the economist will tell us, social security is no longer an insurance program, but an outright subvention. Granted. But arguments against moderate state subsidies depend more and more for their cogency on philosophical and political rather than on economic objections. If it could be demonstrated that the deficit in the operation of the social security program is paralyzing or distorting economic life, the arguments would be economic as well as philosophical. But Mr. J. K. Galbraith and others are correct in maintaining that affluent societies can turn economic tricks impoverished societies cannot; so that the question in America is no longer, "Can the society make up the difference between revenue and income in the social security program?" but *"Should* it?"—a philosophical rather than an economic question. India cannot sustain a social security program for the simple reason that the nation does not have the wherewithal; but the same cannot be said of the United States. I am not saying that social security does not *have* economic consequences—it clearly does, as we shall see; but that the economic case against social security, in our society, appears to be slight.

Concede the fact of a deficit—where does the government get the money? Either a) by taxation (we assume the budget is balanced); or b) by borrowing (budget unbalanced). In the first event, the economic consequence is a levy on the many (all taxpayers) in behalf of the few (the recipients of social security). That levy could presumably have, here and there, marginal economic consequences. In theory, there exists the marginal business concern which, on account of the extra burden upon it traceable to the social security deficit, would fail to make ends meet, and so go bankrupt—a critical economic consequence indeed. But also *in theory,* there is balanced against it the business made marginally profitable by the expenditure of the extra money, put in the hands of the older members of society. Apart from the marginal firm, every business must on account of social security charge a little more, every individual can pay a little less, and economic accommodations are made all along the line. These are serious, or not, depending on their impact on the individual.

Let us assume alternative b) above—that the government borrows the money. To the extent the government can manage to borrow without causing inflation (it is of course technically possible), the economic cost to society is measured by the interest paid on the debt. That interest is raised (barring *ad hoc* appropriations) from existing taxes, based on existing tax patterns. Again the question: is there the marginal taxpayer for whom the derivative levy triggers insolvency? And the complementary question: are there an offsetting number of persons whose income is marginally raised by the expenditure of the money in question?

Finally, assume the government inflates away the debt caused by the social security deficit. The economic consequences? A levy on every dollar, in cash or deposits, the value of which is diluted by the (unearned) increase in the dollars in circulation. The economic consequence is a uniformly depreciated dollar. Economically, the effect can be dire for the men living on a marginal income, which now becomes submarginal.

One can readily see that what results from the insolvency of the federal social security program, however the deficit is provided for, is not, in the American context, severe economic dislocation. Not for so long as the social security deficit represents so small a percentage of the national income.* What does result, whatever way is chosen to make up the deficiency, is a redistribution of income—*to* the social security beneficiary, *from* a) taxpayers in proportion as they are already being taxed (i.e., progressively), or b) all persons with a

---

* In 1957, social security receipts amounted to 7.38 billion dollars, disbursements 7.51 billion dollars. The deficit, 130 million dollars, amounts to .03 per cent of the national income of 440.3 billion dollars. Cost per capita: 73 cents. Projected receipts in 1970, 11.55 billion dollars, disbursements 13.27 billion dollars. Deficit, 1.72 billion dollars.

dollar or more to their name, including the social security beneficiaries themselves, whose own dollars are deflated in value. But the redistribution of income is primarily a subject of philosophical and political interest. The deficit in the federal social security program cannot be shown to have had crucial economic results in this country in the years gone by; but the social security program itself has raised problems of high philosophical importance.

Before going into them, let me say that although I have dealt with the federal social security program as a synecdoche, I am aware that I have come to conclusions based on quantitative evaluation of the costs of social security which would not necessarily be warranted if one were reckoning the cost of the entire apparatus of social welfare in this country. Whereas it is true that federal social security, insofar as it incurs a modest operating deficit, has a negligible economic effect, it is not true that the entire overhead of social welfare has negligible economic effects. Add to social security the billions spent on direct subsidies for farmers, indirect subsidies for certain industries, the insulation of labor from the disciplines of the marketplace; consider the effect of all this on the deployment of a nation's resources and energies, and the economic consequences are certainly considerable, even for a nation with a gross national product in excess of $400 billion. My reason for abstracting social security is two-fold: to begin with, it has an almost unique symbolical significance in American social controversy, where it holds down a position as the quintessence of modern welfarism. Secondly, if it can be shown that the economic consequences of a single federal social service are negligible, then it follows that the economic consequences of a second social service can be negligible; and perhaps a third, and so on. In a word, I am arguing that to a far greater extent than where philosophical values are the point at issue, the economic meaning of a social security measure is quantitatively measurable. A hundred billion dollar economy with federal social security running a deficit of, say, ten million, *can be argued* to have become able to "afford" a further social service with the same contemplated operating deficit (say federal medical insurance) when its earnings are up to two hundred billion. And, as the economy grows to three hundred billion, a federal housing program might become "feasible"—with economic dislocations no greater, proportionately, than they were back in the days when it was only social security.

There are not a few conservative publicists who seem to be applying quantitative criteria to quantitative problems. The social security program has been criticized, among other things, as certain to induce national insolvency. It will not, as presently projected; and it is not likely ever to cause it. It may cause other things, of which I shall treat below, but not that; and one must distinguish. By the same token, a cogent economic evaluation of the economic strain of the aggregate of social services requires reference to the national income and population figures.

4.

But what of the philosophical objections to social security? They are several. I begin with the most insubstantial.

1. *Blanket social security coverage encourages malingering and abuse.* (Tacit premise: That which encourages sloth is philosophically objectionable.)

The conservative emphasis on malingering is inordinate. To be sure, mass malingering can have serious economic consequences. But then it is the economic consequences, rather than the ethical, that one is thereupon called to cope with. If a man abuses an individual's generosity surely it is not generosity that stands indicted; nor would the typical conservative find himself advising anyone, in the future, *not* to be generous. It is prudent to take reasonable precautions against the abuse of a beneficence; but it is not correct to evaluate a beneficence on its abuse-potential. I do not wish to carry the point to extreme; some beneficently conceived systems pose temptations so glaringly irresistible as to bring on an endemic demoralization. The ease with which abortions are secured in Sweden appears to have done less in the way of reducing bastardy (the benevolently conceived objective of the "reforms") than in encouraging promiscuity. These social security laws (or unemployment compensation laws) whose most conspicuous effect is to encourage idleness rather than to mitigate hardship, are not philosophically objectionable; they are, simply, misconceived. In opposing them, one should make the latter point, not the former.

2. *Social security laws are an imposture.* (Tacit premise: They are presented as an "insurance" program. They are not that, in the orthodox sense.) Correct. To the extent the social security program is sold as an "insurance" program, and its "clients" encouraged to think that their employers are paying part of the cost, the program is fraudulent, and let us beware the tolerance of fraud. As we live with it, we do damage to our critical and moral sensibilities.

3. *The social security program is redistributionist in character, since, as we have seen, it implicitly contemplates taking from some in order to give to others.* (Tacit premise: Forcible redistribution is, except in extraordinary situations, ethically indefensible.) Correct. But the redistributionist character of the federal social security program is not its salient characteristic. One does not argue against Foreign Aid on the grounds that one despises Mohammedan polygamy. Redistribution is a corollary effect of social security, and social security is therefore not the indicated battleground for a philosophical assault on redistributionism. Why launch the attack at that point when the enemy resides in plain view elsewhere—in the progressive income tax?

4. *Participation in the social security program is compulsory.* (Tacit premise: Compulsory participation in any enterprise is wrong, because human freedom is diminished.) Wholly correct. A society has the right to impose negative restraints; but positive acts of compli-

153

ance it may exact only in extraordinary situations.* One may not murder, steal, drive drunkenly, commit libel, undress publicly. But there is not, for each of these prohibitions, a corresponding injunction of an affirmative kind. To requite participation in a social enterprise is a fatal habit for a free society to get into. There are times when it must be done. A society may compel its members to serve in the armed forces when that society is clearly threatened. But it must not conscript its citizens except where such a threat is directly posed.

Assuming that the economic survival of the nation depended on unanimous participation in the social security system: would society *then* be entitled to require enrollment of all its citizens? Yes. But *only* if the demonstration could be made; only if it could be shown that the indispensable enterprise, as conceived, could not be executed without unanimous participation; i.e., voluntarily. The argument that the many would, under a voluntary system, find themselves performing sacrifices in behalf of the few (the alleged injustice on which the case against the right-to-work laws is based) is not applicable here, because social security payments are not "sacrifices." They are payments against a future service. Those who do not enroll in the program do not make the payments, but neither do the benefits inure to them.

I conclude that the most serious argument against the federal social security laws of the United States has to do with its compulsory character.

But, hark, now, the difficulties of the conservative demonstration. And let me be clear on a crucial point,

* John Stuart Mill put it uncompromisingly: ". . . one very simple principle [is] . . . entitled to govern absolutely the dealings of society with the individual in the way of compulsion and control . . . That principle is, that the sole end for which mankind are warranted, individually or collectively, in interfering with the liberty of action of any of their number, is self-protection. That the only purpose for which power can be rightfully exercised over any member of a civilized community, against his will, is to prevent harm to others. His own good, either physical or moral, is not a sufficient warrant . . ." *Utilitarianism, On Liberty, and Representative Government* (New York, 1914), p. 72.

that I distinguish sharply in this chapter between the rightness, *sub specie aeternitatis,* of the conservative position, and the cogency of its appeal to a presumptively right-minded body politic. To begin with, if one assumes that the absence of organized political opposition to social security laws faithfully reflects the degree of public satisfaction with the laws or at least the low temperature of public dissatisfaction (a very reasonable assumption), we are bound to conclude that very few people, if given the opportunity, would opt for exclusion from the social security program. It is a very small minority, in a word, who are being coerced; and the majority is concerned with oppression only in the academic way in which majorities tend to concern themselves with the idiosyncratic grievances of minorities against measures commonly understood to be beneficial to majority and minority alike.

Bear in mind, I speak of the failure of the conservative demonstration. A society can be organized, as ours is, around immutable and highly explicit postulates; but it is, in practice, unlikely to submit to them when submission appears nonsensical. A libertarian theorist has no difficulty in clinching his theoretical case against the social security laws—he has merely to state simply that the program has the effect of abridging a freedom unnecessarily. But the flesh-and-blood dissident has earthier problems. John Stuart Mill, the muse of Pure Freedom of Opinion, maintained that so categorical is the right of dissent that the dissident must be protected even from the slightest suggestion of the "moral coercion of public opinion." That is the simon-pure theory. But try to prevent a community from expressing impatience with, let us say, a local Communist. For that matter, try to prevent John Stuart Mill Professors of Political Science from visiting a little genteel moral coercion on the thick skull of that perverse reactionary in their department who believes that . . .

The oppressed minority, if it is asking for relief by the majority, must find a way of stating its case compellingly. Otherwise, the majority is not likely to inconvenience itself. If the majority, moreover, feels that the complaints of the minority are frivolous, it is not likely to go out of its way to accommodate us, however conclusively we establish our solidarity with such supraconstitutional deities as John Stuart Mill.

Why? The answer does not lie in the simple fact that very few people are opposed to the coercive character of social security. Very few people take advantage of the freedom of speech, is that not so? If a law were imposed limiting the right of free speech, how many people would be affected? I should guess thousands, not tens of thousands, for there are not so many of us engaged in writing, or speaking our heterodoxies in public. But all of us would rise, as one man, to protest the passage of any such law, because we are adequately trained to resist impingements on that freedom. We are not, however, adequately trained to resist other restrictions, even those that affect many more members of the community than an impingement of free speech would do. Pass a law levying an additional tax for social security, and millions are affected. The fact that they acquiesce in the appropriation of their pennies does not alter the fact that they now have fewer pennies to spend, and that their freedom is, accordingly, diminished. Conservatives have failed to alert the community to the interconnection between economic freedom and—freedom. No government would dare be so abusive as ours is of our economic freedoms if we were alive to the relationship. It is a part of the conservative intuition that economic freedom is the most precious temporal freedom, for the reason that it alone gives to each one of us, in our comings and goings in our complex society, sovereignty— and over that part of existence in which by far the most choices have in fact to be made, and in which it is possible to make choices, involving oneself, without damage to other people. And for the further reason that without economic freedom, political and other freedoms are likely to be taken from us.

At the moment the nation is very much attracted by the sophism of Professor Galbraith, to which I have alluded before, namely that we are not as consumers really free, inasmuch as we are pawns of the advertising agencies. To begin with, there is the factual exaggeration (the perverseness of the American buying public is the despair of advertising agencies); but even then, what meaning has the generalization for us? Of *course* we are influenced by others in what we do and think, and sometimes we are influenced in the direction of making choices that are hard to defend objectively. Professor Galbraith is horrified by the number of Americans who have bought cars with tail fins on them, and I am horrified by the number of Americans who take seriously the proposals of Mr. Galbraith. But whereas he would, by preempting the people's money, take the power from them to put tail fins on their cars, I should be hesitant (though I would prefer the society with lots of tail fins to the society with lots of Dr. Galbraith's proposals running around dangerously) to preempt the people's money, even though part of it is due to be spent on purchasing books by Dr. Galbraith—which, by the way, have been prodigiously advertised.

Let the individual keep his dollar—however few he is able to save—and he can indulge his taste (and never mind who had a role in shaping it) in houses, in doctors, in education, in groceries, in entertainment, in culture, in religion; give him the right of free speech or the right to go to the polling booth, and at best he contributes to a collective determination, contributes as a general rule an exiguous voice. Give me the right to spend my dollars as I see fit—to devote them, as I see fit, to travel, to food, to learning, to taking pleasure, to polemicizing, and, if I must make the choice, I will surrender you my political franchise in trade, confident that by the transaction, assuming the terms of the contract are that no political decision affecting my sovereignty over my dollar can be made, I shall have augmented my dominance over my own affairs.

That is the demonstration, surely, that the conservatives need to make, before we are overwhelmed; but how pitiful have been our efforts, how tragic our failure.

How vulnerable our desire for economic freedom to the devastating indictment of materialism. It is widely felt that the right of property is a rich-man's concern, that the Cadillac he hungers after is the fullest expression of that freedom. How widely it is assumed that societies can, without damage to the metaphysical base of freedom, do away with Cadillacs. Thus have they framed the argument: you have nothing to lose, by our depredations on economic freedom, but a few Cadillacs. It is as if we asked them to prove the value of free speech even to the few who exercise it, by citing only the works of Gerald L. K. Smith.

It follows why conservatism has failed to hold the line for freedom, whether in behalf of dissident social security subscribers, farmers at loggerheads with Agriculture Department bureaucrats, workers conscripted into labor unions, or businessmen struggling against the massive harassment of regulatory agencies. Conservatives have not "proved" to the satisfaction either of the public or of the academy that the moderate* welfare state has paralyzing economic or political consequences for the affluent* society. Our insistence that the economic comeuppance is just around the corner (not *this* corner, *that* one. No, not *that* one, *that* one over *there* . . .) has lost to conservatism public confidence in its economic expertise. And on the matter of liberty, conservatives have not been persuasive (because of the failure I speak of) in their contention that the freedoms they have been forced by the welfare state to do without add up to humiliation, let alone privation.**

---

* Vague adjectives—dangerous, I concede, in this kind of analysis. I understand a "moderate" welfare state to be one that addresses itself to the physical necessities of life (as distinct from the kind of omniconcerned welfarism that, e.g., Professor J. K. Galbraith would visit upon us); and by "affluent" I mean the society that can relieve physical distress out of earned surplus, without doing organic damage to the society's economic mechanism.

** The obvious exception is the rich man, whose problem is distinctive and, I use the word deliberately, pathetic. The rich man is unmistakably the victim of ideology. In an affluent society, we do not need to tax the millionaire 90 per cent, or his estate 70 per cent. The money that comes in to the treasury, at these levels, is

The individual who proclaims it an impingement upon his freedom to be required to pay two per cent of his salary into a social security fund will be fretted over by the community about as much as the community, left to its own devices, would worry about the professors who pronounce it an affront on their dignity to be required to sign a non-Communist oath. At the latter's disposal there are great echo chambers (the highly mobilized civil liberties lobby, the professional academic associations, and so on) which if they do not succeed in persuading the majority to be on their side, give the impression that they have, which is almost as good; and so they have their way, with state and national legislatures. But there is no significant lobby to go into action to defend the rights of the libertarian when concern is with property rights, because of the elementary failure to establish the nexus between individual freedom and property rights. Until the objection to involuntary participation in social security reifies in the public mind as something more than a ritualistic exercise in libertarian crankiness, we are not going to set the nation marching to our rescue.

5.

The temptation is to measure freedom subjectively. But it is very dangerous indeed to cede to a society the right to declare what are and what are not the freedoms worth exercising. To be sure, one man may not feel free unless he can render his political views without let or hindrance. Another may put the highest value on his freedom to walk through the streets late at night. A

---

negligible, measured against the budget. If the federal individual income tax were cut to a 50 per cent top, the U.S. would have lost in revenue in 1955, a total of $734 million. In America, the rich man is no longer the natural antagonist of the people. The demagogues and egalitarians need to work hard to keep lit the fires of egalitarianism and envy. A recent (Gallup) poll indicates that the majority of Americans a) believe the income tax goes no higher than 35 per cent, and b) believe the tax *should* go no higher than 25 per cent.

third may care principally about his freedom to shoot ducks. Freedom belongs also to the eccentric—that much we should be quite firm about. It may be eccentric to complain about being docked a few dollars a week for social security; but how far can we go, if we deal thus cavalierly with the minority's freedoms, without changing the very nature of the voluntarist society?

What all conservatives in this country fear, and have plenty of reason to fear, is the loss of freedom by attrition. It is therefore for the most realistic reasons, as well as those of principle, that we must resist every accretion of power by the state, even while guarding our rhetoric against such exaggerations as equating social security with slavery. The conservative rhetoric has here and there run ahead of events. Even though I myself take the gloomy view that our society is marching toward totalitarianism, I should not go so far as to say that America is not now, as societies go, free—however gravely I view the restrictions on freedom implicit in, e.g., the progressive income tax, the ban on religious teaching in public schools, the union shop, the FEPC's, the farm laws, etc. Freedom is *not* indivisible. The more freedom the better, which means that some freedom is better than none at all, and more than some is better still. The conservative must, therefore, guard against the self-discrediting generalization that our society is no longer "free," while insisting, as implacably as the liberal does every time a Communist is harassed by a disciplinary law, that not an appropriation is passed by the legislatures, but that our freedom is diminished.

The failure of the conservative demonstration in political affairs rests primarily on our failure to convince that the establishment of the welfare state entails the surrender, bit by bit, of minor freedoms which, added together, can alter the very shape of our existence.

The tendencies of liberalism are every day more visibly coercive, as the social planners seek more and more brazenly to impose their preferences upon us. Here, I believe, is a practical distinction at which conservatives should hammer hard—the distinction between the kind of welfarism that turns dollars over to people, and that which turns services over to them. The former kind is embodied in such legislation as social security, unemployment compensation, and old age assistance. The latter in federal aid to education, to housing, to rural electrification, small business, etc.; and the proposed "insurance" programs, e.g., health, accident, etc.

In the first instance, the recipient of the money is free to allocate it according to his own lights, to satisfy his own needs and pleasures according to his own estimate of their priority. There are the obvious perils, that he will stress whiskey rather than milk, television over education; but these are the perils of liberty, with which conservatives are prepared to live. In making money grants, as distinguished from the other kind (for instance public housing subsidies), the government is prevented from taking active control of industries or social services, or from having the deciding hand in the creation or development of social or service institutions. I judge this to be significant, because as long as one is free to spend the money with reference to one's desires, the government's control is at least once removed. And then at the tactical level, the longer one can hold off or slow down such grandiose ambitions of the welfarists as free health services, expanded public housing, government aid to airports, highways, schools, Olympic-game sites, the more difficult it will be to establish the necessity for the government's undertaking such enterprises. The arguments of the affluent society work in two ways: as we become richer we can indeed devote more attention to economic non-essentials. But as the people become richer we can also leave more and more to them to do out of their own resources, can we not? Surely the argument for socialized medicine in India is more compelling than the argument for socialized medicine in America. That is to say, if the relevant standard is, How many Indians, as opposed to Americans, can afford to pay their own medical bills? Granted, the question is left begging. Where is the government of India going to raise the money to pay for the hospitals, health centers, doctors, nurses and equipment we can all agree are urgently needed in India? The problem having been pondered over in the context of economic realities, the wise man will conclude that the best way to make medicine widely available it to make wealth widely available, and in turn the best way to do that is to liberate the economic system from statist impositions.*

I think the conservative has the best of the argument when he maintains that security does not equal freedom, even though he admits that freedom is also for the eccentric. Objective standards of freedom must not be lost sight of, in our indulgence of the eccentric. If a man feels free in prison, we must simultaneously acknowledge his right to feel free, and declare that he is not free. If the people announce that they feel freer by virtue of the securities extended by the welfare state, we must be prepared to concede what they authoritatively tell us about their state of mind—yet insist, doggedly, that we strive after an objectively free society. If the people are willing to accept substitutes for freedom, that may be styled as their "right." There is no effective means of disputing man's right to self-deception, and certainly there is no questioning his capacity for it; but spinach remains spinach, and on this point one must speak plainly. The conservative must struggle to impart to the popular imagination the great insight into the nature of freedom which, because it was kept vividly in mind in the early years of our nation, preserved the climate of freedom.

I add a note of caution: though the conservative must say that freedom is freedom, not anything else that suits someone just as well, he must guard against saying that the kind of security purchased by, e.g., the social secu-

---

* J. K. Galbraith seems to agree, though he says it in a roundabout way: "An affluent society, that is also both compassionate and rational, would, no doubt, secure to all who needed it the minimum income essential for decency and comfort . . . When poverty was a majority phenomenon [as it now is in, e.g., India—W.F.B.] such action could not be afforded. A poor society . . . *had* [my emphasis —W.F.B.] to enforce the rule that the person who did not work could not eat. And possibly it was [even] justified in the added cruelty of applying the rule to those who could not work or whose efficiency was far below par."

rity laws, is an "illusory" security. That is an observation that makes men and women who are subjected to it very impatient, and rightly so. To be sure, all "security" is illusory; but unless we have more specific things in mind, we surely do not want to trouble to make the point that that which is illusory is illusory. As far as state welfare is concerned, there is a long enough historical record of it to establish that relatively affluent societies given to a measure of state welfarism *can* extend their economic lives over an impressive period of time without collapsing from exhaustion. The social security law and related welfare laws have been in operation for about twenty years, and in them many people have in fact found security. (I am not of course suggesting these same people would not have found security elsewhere, had the government stayed out of the picture.) During those twenty years we spent 650 billion dollars on national defense, so that the coordinate economic strain on our society was enormous and, let us hope, unusual. *Even* so, our economy has not collapsed—though it almost certainly has been damaged. It is quite possibly true that through such measures as federal social security we sow seeds that could lead to economic destruction; but then it is also true that being born with Original Sin is a poor way to start out in life. Social security will *not* necessarily bring economic collapse— it is merely a step in the wrong direction; a departure from sound principles of government. To insist doctrinally that it will bring disaster is to weaken the case for conservatism, and make difficult the conservative demonstration.

6.

Mr. Peregrine Worsthorne of England, who wrestles eloquently with the problem of conservative leadership in his own country, has made known his position on the welfare state,* and it is in line with that of our

---

* "Conservative Thoughts Out of Season," *Encounter,* London, August, 1958.

own New Conservatives. He writes of the necessity of strengthening England's middle class, but warns that any move to do so must be "only a part of a wider program with a national appeal. Essential to such a program . . . is loyalty to the basic features of the Welfare State which, by reducing class antagonisms, creates precisely the right climate of opinion for strengthening the middle class. Those conservatives who would dismantle the Welfare State overlook the fact that a secure working class, far from being a challenge to the middle class, is its indispensable condition. For only if the many are spared economic hardship can the few expect to enjoy economic and social privilege . . . the concept of welfare must be staunchly defended. Nor, given an expanding economy, will this impose a crippling economic burden, and those conservatives who pretend it will are doing their own cause unnecessary damage."

I am not absolutely sure I know what Mr. Worsthorne is saying. Is he telling us—perhaps it is true—that the working class will hereinafter lay down the conditions of life in England? The class question in this country is not so tidy, but the problem is there. Universal suffrage broke up the conservative society. And since the enlargement of the electorate tends to be an irreversible political process, the means are not visible by which the voters can be estopped from substituting political for economic means of self-aggrandizement; from redistributing. But are we not to *look* for the means?

And does Mr. Worsthorne mean by "loyalty" what others mean by it? I should think conservatives should be loyal in their *opposition* to the welfare state, for the reasons I have touched upon; even while recognizing that for the time being, at least, political opposition to deeply imbedded welfarist carbuncles is futile. But how is the conservative politician of tomorrow going to oppose the *next* suggested federal enterprise, if not by adducing reasons of a principled kind—which apply with equal cogency to existing measures, whose justification he is supposed to be loyal to? How oppose free false teeth (I almost said compulsory false teeth) or free psychoanalysis (compulsory?) without making a case against coercive social security?

Mr. Worsthorne is correct in suggesting that whatever tactical opportunities the welfare state accidentally delivers to conservatives (e.g., a pacified lower class), we should proceed to exploit. And it may be, even, that he senses correctly the mood in England: that so long as conservatives inveigh against the existing welfare state as though they would, given the opportunity, dismantle it, the working class will see to it that they are never given the power. But Mr. Worsthorne must not ask us to suppress the critical intelligence—and nothing less than that will do, to instill in us a loyalty to the welfare state. And, of course, we have dreams to dream.

The Conservative Framework and Modern Realities

AN AFTERWORD

. . . an essay such as this is far more important for what it destroys—or to speak more accurately, for the destruction which it crystallizes, since the ultimate enemy of myth is circumstance—than for what it creates. This is sharply at odds with the conventional wisdom. The latter sets great store by what it calls constructive criticism. And it reserves its scorn for what it is likely to term a purely destructive or negative position. In this, as so often, it manifests a sound instinct for self-preservation.

J. K. GALBRAITH, *The Affluent Society.*

UP WHERE FROM LIBERALISM? There is no conservative political manifesto which, as we make our faltering way, we can consult, confident that it will point a sure finger in the direction of the good society. Indeed, sometimes the conservative needle appears to be jumping about as on a disoriented compass. My professional life is lived in an office battered by every pressure of contemporary conservatism. Some of the importunities upon a decent American conservatism are outrageous, or appear so to me, at any rate. (*"We should have high tariffs because the farmers have high subsidies, and they shouldn't, by the way."*) Some are pathological (*"Alaska is being prepared as a mammoth concentration camp for pro-McCarthyites"*). Some are deeply mystical (*"The state can do no good."* My answer: it can arrest Communists, can't it?); some ambitiously spiritual (*"Conservatism has no extrinsic significance except in relation to religion"*). Some urge the schematization of conservatism. (*"What passes for conservatism these days is nothing more than sentimentality and nostalgia. Let us give it structure . . ."*); or the opposite (*"Beware the ideologization of conservatism."*).

Still, for all the confusion and contradiction, I venture to say it is possible to talk about "the conservative position" and mean something by it. At the political level, conservatives are bound together for the most part by negative response to liberalism; but altogether too much is made of that fact. Negative action is not necessarily of negative value. Political freedom's principal value is negative in character. The people are politically stirred principally by the necessity for negative affirmations. Cincinnatus was a farmer before he took up his sword, and went back to farming after wielding some highly negative strokes upon the pates of those who sought to make positive changes in his way of life.

The weakness of American conservatives does not reduce neatly to the fact that some want tariffs, others not. Dr. Robert Oppenheimer was much taken during the 1950's by what goes by the name of "complementarity," a notion having to do with revised relationships in the far reaches of philosophical thought, where "opposites" come under a single compass, and fuse into workable philosophical and physical unities. No doubt Physicist Oppenheimer was sticking an irreverent finger in the higher chemistry of metaphysics: but his theory, like the Hegelian synthesis, served to remind us that there is almost always conceivable the vantage point from which the seemingly incongruous, the apparently contradictory, can be viewed in harmony. A navigator for whom two lighthouses can mark extreme points of danger relative to his present position, knows that by going back and making a wholly different approach, the two lighthouses will fuse together to form a single object to the vision, confirming the safety of his position. They are then said to be "in range."

There is a point from which opposition to the social security laws and a devout belief in social stability are in range; as also a determined resistance to the spread of world Communism—and a belief in political non-interventionism; a disgust with the results of modern education—and sympathy for the individual educational requirements of the individual child; a sympathetic understanding of the spiritual essence of human existence—and a desire to delimit religious influence in political affairs; a patriotic concern for the nation and its culture—and a genuine respect for the integrity and differences of other peoples' culture; a militant concern for the Negro—and a belief in decentralized political power even though, on account of it, the Negro is sometimes victimized; a respect for the omnicompetence of the free marketplace—and the knowledge of the necessity for occupational interposition. There is a position from which these views are "in range"; and that is the position, generally speaking, where conservatives now find themselves on the political chart. Our most serious challenge is to restore principles—the right principles; the principles liberalism has abused, forsaken, and replaced with "principles" that have merely a methodological content—our challenge is to restore principles to public affairs.

I mentioned in the opening pages of this book that what was once a healthy American pragmatism has deteriorated into a wayward relativism. It is one thing to make the allowances to reality that reality imposes, to take advantage of the current when the current moves in your direction, while riding at anchor at ebb tide. But it is something else to run before political or historical impulses merely because fractious winds begin to blow, and to dismiss resistance as foolish, or perverse idealism. And it is supremely wrong, intellectually and morally, to abandon the norms by which it becomes possible, viewing a trend, to pass judgment upon it; without which judgment we cannot know whether to yield, or to fight.

Are we to fight the machine? Can conservatism assimilate it? Whittaker Chambers once wrote me that "the rock-core of the Conservative Position can be held realistically only if Conservatism will accommodate itself to the needs and hopes of the masses—needs and hopes which like the masses themselves, are the product of machines."

It is true that the masses have asserted themselves, all over the world; have revolted, Ortega said, perceiving the revolutionary quality of the cultural convulsion. The question: how can conservatism accommodate revolution? Can the revolutionary essence be extravasated and be made to diffuse harmlessly in the network of capillaries that rushes forward to accommodate its explosive force? Will the revolt of the masses moderate when the lower class is risen, when science has extirpated misery, and the machine has abolished poverty? Not if the machines themselves are irreconcilable, as Mr. Chambers seemed to suggest when he wrote that ". . . of course, our fight is with machines," adding: "A conservatism that cannot face the facts of the machine and mass production, and its consequences in government and politics, is foredoomed to futility and petulance. A conservatism that allows for them has an eleventh-hour chance of rallying what is sound in the West."

What forms must this accommodation take? *The welfare state!* is the non-Communist answer one mostly hears. It is necessary, we are told, to comprehend the interdependence of life in an industrial society, and the social consequences of any action by a single part of it, on other parts. Let the steel workers go on strike, and spark-plug salesmen will in due course be out of work. There must be laws to mitigate the helplessness of the individual link in the industrial chain that the machine has built.

What can conservatism do? Must it come to terms with these realities? "To live is to maneuver [Mr. Chambers continued]. The choices of maneuver are now visibly narrow. In the matter of social security, for example, the masses of Americans, like the Russian peasants in 1918, are signing the peace with their feet. I worked the hay load last night against the coming rain —by headlights, long after dark. I know the farmer's case for the machine and for the factory. And I know, like the cut of hay-bale cords in my hands, that a conservatism that cannot find room in its folds for these actualities is a conservatism that is not a political force, or even a twitch: it has become a literary whimsy."

Indeed. The machine must be accepted, and conservatives must not live by programs that were written as though the machine did not exist, or could be made to go away; that is the proper kind of realism. The big question is whether the essential planks of conservatism were anachronized by the machine; the big answer is that they were not. "Those who remain in the world, if they will not surrender on its terms, must maneuver within its terms [said Mr. Chambers]. That is what conservatives must decide: how much to give in order to survive at all; how much to give in order not to give up the basic principles. And, of course, that results in a dance along a precipice. Many will drop over, and, always, the cliff-dancers will hear the screaming curses of those who fall, or be numbed by the sullen silence of those, nobler souls perhaps, who will not join in the dance." We cliff-dancers, resolved not to withdraw into a petulant solitude, or let ourselves fall over the cliff into liberalism, must do what maneuvering we can, and come up with a conservative program that speaks to our time.

It is the chronic failure of liberalism that it obliges circumstance—because it has an inadequate discriminatory apparatus which might cause it to take any other course. There are unemployed in Harlan County? *Rush them aid.* New Yorkers do not want to pay the cost of subways? *Get someone else to pay it.* Farmers do not want to leave the land? *Let them till it, buy and destroy the produce.* Labor unions demand the closed shop? *It is theirs.* Inflation goes forward in all industrial societies? *We will have continued inflation.* Communism is in control behind the Iron Curtain? *Coexist with it.* The tidal wave of industrialism will sweep in the welfare state? *Pull down the sea walls.*

Conservatism must insist that while the will of man is limited in what it can do, it can do enough to make over the face of the world; and that the question that must always be before us is, What shape should the world take, given modern realities? How can technology hope to invalidate conservatism? Freedom, individuality, the sense of community, the sanctity of the family, the supremacy of the conscience, the spiritual view of life—can these verities be transmuted by the advent of tractors and adding machines? These have had a smashing social effect upon us, to be sure. They have created a vortex into which we are being drawn as though irresistibly; but that, surely, is because the principles by which we might have made anchor have not been used, not because of their insufficiency or proven inadaptability. "Technology has succeeded in extracting just about the last bit of taste from a loaf of bread," columnist Murray Kempton once told me spiritedly. "And when we get peacetime use of atomic energy, we'll succeed in getting *all* the taste out!"

How can one put the problem more plainly? I assume by now Mrs. Kempton has gone to the archives, dusted off an ancient volume, and learned how to bake homemade bread. And Lo! the bread turns out to be as easy to make as before, tastes as good as before, and the machine age did not need to be roasted at an *auto-da-fé* to make it all possible. A conservative solution to *that* problem. But when the atom does to politics what it threatens to bread, what *then* is the solution? Can one make homemade freedom, under the eyes of an omnipotent state that has no notion of, or tolerance for, the flavor of freedom?

Freedom and order and community and justice in an age of technology: that is the contemporary challenge of political conservatism. How to do it, how to live with mechanical harvesters and without socialized agriculture. The direction we must travel requires a broadmindedness that, in the modulated age, strikes us as antiquarian, and callous. As I write there is mass suffering in Harlan County, Kentucky, where coal mining has become unprofitable, and a whole community is desolate. The liberal solution is: immediate and sustained federal subsidies. The conservative, breasting the emotional surf, will begin by saying that it was many years ago foreseeable that coal mining in Harlan County was becoming unprofitable, that the humane course would have been to face up to that realism by permitting the marketplace, through the exertion of economic pressures of mounting intensity, to require resettlement. That was not done for the coal miners (they were shielded from reality by a combination of state and union aid)—any more than it is now being done for marginal farmers; so that we are face-to-face with an acute emergency for which there is admittedly no thinkable alternative to immediate relief—if necessary (though it is not) by the federal government; otherwise, by the surrounding communities, or the state of Kentucky. But having made arrangements for relief, what then? Will the grandsons of the Harlan coal miners be mining coal, to be sold to the government at a pegged price, all this to spare today's coal miners the ordeal of looking for other occupations?

The Hoover Commission on government reorganization unearthed several years ago a little rope factory in Boston, Massachusetts, which had been established by the federal government during the Civil War to manufacture the textile specialties the Southern blockade had caused to be temporarily scarce. There it was, ninety years after Appomattox, grinding out the same specialties, which are bought by the government, and then sold at considerable loss. "Liquidate the plant," the Hoover Commission was getting ready to recommend. Whereupon a most influential Massachusetts Senator, Mr. John F. Kennedy, interceded. "You cannot," he informed a member of the Commission, "do so heinous a thing. The plant employs 136 persons, whose only skill is in making this specialty." "Very well then," said the spokesman for the Commission, anxious to cooperate. "Suppose we recommend to the Government that the factory retain in employment every single present employee until he quits, retires, or dies—but on the understanding that none of them is to be replaced. That way we can at least look forward to the eventual liquidation of the plant. Otherwise, there will be 136 people making useless specialties generations hence; an unreasonable legacy of the Civil War."

The Senator was unappeased. What a commotion the proposal would cause in the textile-specialty enclave in Boston! The solution, he warned the Commission, was intolerable, and he would resist it with all his prodigious political might.

The relationship of forces being what it is, the factory continues to operate at full force.

To be sure, a great nation can indulge its little extravagances, as I have repeatedly stressed; but a long enough series of little extravagances, as I have also said, can add up to a stagnating if not a crippling economic overhead. What is disturbing about the Civil War factory incident is first the sheer stupidity of the thing, second the easy victory of liberal sentimentalism over reason. Subsidies are the form that modern circuses tend to take, and, as ever, the people are unaware that it is they who pay for the circuses.

But closing down the useless factories—a general war on featherbedding—is the correct thing to do, if it is correct to cherish the flavor of freedom and economic sanity. There is a sophisticated argument that has to do with the conceivable economic beneficences of pyramid building, and of hiring men to throw rocks out into the sea. But even these proposals, when advanced rhetorically by Lord Keynes, were meliorative and temporary in concept: the idea was to put the men to work *until* the regenerative juices of the economy had done their work. Now we wake to the fact that along the line we abandoned our agreement to abide, as a general rule, by the determinations of the marketplace. We once believed that useless textile workers and useless coal miners and useless farmers—and useless carriagemakers and pony expressmen—should search out other means of employment.

It is the dawning realization that, under the economics of illusion, pyramid building is becoming a major economic enterprise in America, that has set advanced liberals to finding more persuasive ways to dispose of the time of the textile specialty workers. And their solution—vide Galbraith—is great social enterprises, roads, schools, slum clearance, national parks. The thesis of the Affluent Society is that simple. We have 1) an earned surplus, 2) unemployment, 3) "social imbalance." (I.e., too many cars, not enough roads; too much carbon monoxide, not enough air purification; too many children, not enough classrooms.) So let the government 1) take over the extra money, 2) use it to hire the unemployed, and 3) set them to restoring the social balance, i.e., to building parks, schools, roads.

The program prescribed by Mr. Galbraith is unacceptable, conservatives would agree. Deal highhandedly as he would have us do with the mechanisms of the marketplace, and the mechanisms will bind. Preempt the surplus of the people, and surpluses will dwindle. Direct politically the economic activity of a nation, and the economy will lose its capacity for that infinite responsiveness to individual tastes that gives concrete expression to the individual will in material matters. Centralize the political function, and you will lose touch with reality, for the reality is an intimate and individualized relationship between individuals and those among whom they live; and the abstractions of wide-screen social draftsmen will not substitute for it. Stifle the economic sovereignty of the individual by spending his dollars for him, and you stifle his freedom. Socialize the individual's surplus and you socialize his spirit and creativeness; you cannot paint the *Mona Lisa* by assigning one dab each to a thousand painters.

Conservatives do not deny that technology poses

enormous problems; they insist only that the answers of liberalism create worse problems than those they set out to solve. Conservatives cannot be blind, or give the appearance of being blind, to the dismaying spectacle of unemployment, or any other kind of suffering. But conservatives can insist that the statist solution to the problem is inadmissible. It is not the single conservative's responsibility or right to draft a concrete program— merely to suggest the principles that should frame it.

What then *is* the indicated course of action? It is to maintain and wherever possible enhance the freedom of the individual to acquire property and dispose of that property in ways that he decides on. To deal with unemployment by eliminating monopoly unionism, featherbedding, and inflexibilities in the labor market, and be prepared, where residual unemployment persists, to cope with it locally, placing the political and humanitarian responsibility on the lowest feasible political unit. Boston can surely find a way to employ gainfully its 136 textile specialists—and its way would be very different, predictably, from Kentucky's with the coal miners; and let them be different. Let the two localities experiment with different solutions, and let the natural desire of the individual for more goods, and better education, and more leisure, find satisfaction in individual encounters with the marketplace, in the growth of private schools, in the myriad economic and charitable activities which, because they took root in the individual imagination and impulse, take organic form. And then let us see whether we are better off than we would be living by decisions made between nine and five in Washington office rooms, where the oligarchs of the Affluent Society sit, allocating complaints and solutions to communities represented by pins on the map.

Is that a program? Call it a No-Program, if you will, but adopt it for your very own. I will not cede more power to the state. I will not willingly cede more power to anyone, not to the state, not to General Motors, not to the CIO. I will hoard my power like a miser, resisting every effort to drain it away from me. I will then use *my* power, as *I* see fit. I mean to live my life an obedient man, but obedient to God, subservient to the wisdom of my ancestors; never to the authority of political truths arrived at yesterday at the voting booth. That is a program of sorts, is it not?

It is certainly program enough to keep conservatives busy, and liberals at bay. And the nation free.

INDEX